the book of
if

the book of

Ri

the book of
if

questions for the
games of life and love

Evelyn McFarlane and James Saywell
Illustrations by James Saywell

QUALITY PAPERBACK BOOK CLUB
NEW YORK

The Book of If
Questions for the Games of Life and Love

If ... (Questions for the Game of Life)
Copyright © 1995 by Evelyn McFarlane and James Saywell

If ^{2} ... (500 More Questions for the Game of Life)
Copyright © 1996 by Evelyn McFarlane and James Saywell

If ^{3} ... (Questions for the Game of Love)
Copyright © 1997 by Evelyn McFarlane and James Saywell

Printed in the United States of America

contents

If...

(Questions for the Game of Life)

If is the ultimate book about fantasy. Each of its questions is meant to spark and tantalize the imagination. They are a celebration of the human spirit, which loves to dream and needs to hope, but which can also fear and even grow angry. Our ability to imagine is the remarkable gift we have been given to lead us into joy and aspiration and out of despair or sadness, because common to all of us is the idea that there could be a different world, perhaps a better one.

How many times a day do we say, "If only . . ."? If we could create the perfect life, the perfect city, the perfect home, the perfect job, the perfect mate. We all fantasize, and we all dream. We dream of perfection, money, revenge, glory, change. We fantasize about both good and evil, about winning and losing, about our past and future. Fantasies are what inspire us all; to work, marry, raise families, create, improve our world. It is why we lose ourselves in books, go to movies, watch television, go to the ballgame and on vacation. We dreamed as children and we dream now because without our fantasies we would be lost. We imagine in order to learn, to understand, to strive, to attempt, to predict, to avoid, to correct, to describe, to solve.

This book is also a game. It was born of many dinner parties and gatherings, when just to throw out a provocative question and ask for each person's answer always led to the most surprising and fascinating discussions. Every time, a kind of synergetic and addictive momentum took over as answers led to other related questions, reasons were demanded, disagreements were unleashed, conditions were imposed, other's answers were predicted, and inevitably those involved were startled by the responses, at times even their own. No matter who is present it seems to be irresistible, whether we are at a flagging party, on a long car or plane ride, among a group of students, within a family, or alone with someone very close to us. It is infectious and fascinating to watch and take part in.

Of course implicit in every question is "why?" In some sense it is like taking the pulse of a moment in time, or a group of friends, to see what we believe in; to see what world we envision. Whether they are read randomly or in sequence, the responses these questions elicit can lead to extraordinary offshoots; other related questions will occur, and variations on these, and attached caveats and conditions "customize" the original list depending on who is there to play. Because everybody, old or young, fat or thin, intelligent or not, from one culture or another, has the ability and inclination to wonder.

And so, aside from the truths that are revealed, the contemplation that is provoked, the confidence or anxiety that surfaces, the self-knowledge that results, or the understanding that might be gained, above all we hope that asking these questions inspires optimism, since no matter who or what we really are, we share the ability to travel together the unpredictable journey of the imagination, which leads us through the wonderful game of life.

If you were to be granted one wish, what would it be?

If you could spend one whole night alone with anyone in the world who is currently alive, who would you select?

If you could spend one whole night alone with anyone in history, who would you choose?

If you could physically transport yourself to any place in the world at this moment, where would you go?

If you could have lived through any war in history (without actually fighting in it), which would it be?

If you could eliminate any one type of insect permanently from the earth, what would you get rid of?

If you had to eliminate a single type of animal forevermore, which would you choose?

If you could have an elegant dinner alone with anyone presently alive, whether you know them or not, who would you want it to be?

If you could alter one physical characteristic of your mate, what would you change?

—————◆—————

If you could dine alone with anyone from any period in history, which person would it be?

—————◆—————

If you could, in retrospect, change one thing about your childhood, what would it be?

—————◆—————

If you could have any room in the world become your bedroom from now on, which room would you choose?

7

If you could change one thing in the world right now, what would you alter?

If you had to assassinate one famous person who is alive right now, who would it be, and how would you do it?

If you could permanently alter one thing about your physical appearance, what would you change?

If you could have stopped aging at any point in your life up to the present, how old would you want to remain?

8

If you could inherit a comfortable home in any city in the world that you could use but not sell, where would you want it to be?

If you could inherit a vacation home anywhere in the world in which you could spend one month a year, but that you could never sell, where would it be?

If you could suddenly possess an extraordinary talent in one of the arts, what would you like it to be?

If you could be instantly fluent in one other language that you currently do not read or speak, which would it be?

9

If you could have permanent possession of any single object in the world, what would you want it to be?

If you could have had the starring role in one film already made, which movie would you pick?

If you could return for one year to one age in your life, knowing what you know now, to relive that year as you wish, which year would you go back to?

If you had to identically repeat any single year of your life to date, without changing a thing, which year would you relive?

10

If you could be sculpted by any artist in history, who would you choose?

If you were to have your entire wardrobe designed for you by a single clothing designer for the rest of your life, who would you select?

If you were to be stranded forever on a desert island and could have only one book to read, which would you want?

If you could say one sentence to the current pope, what would it be?

If you could have one person from history live his or her full life over again, starting now, who would you pick?

If you could have personally witnessed one event in history, what would you want to have seen?

If one of your parents was to be a famous person from any time in history, who would you want them to be?

If you could receive one small package this very moment, who would it be from and what would be in it?

12

If you could own one painting from any collection in the world but were not allowed to sell it, which work of art would you select?

If you could have chosen your own first name, other than your current one, what would it be?

If you could have seduced one person that you knew in your lifetime (but didn't), who would you select?

If you were instantly able to play one musical instrument perfectly that you never have played before, what would it be?

If you were to be stranded forever on a tropical island with one platonic friend only, in whose company would you want to spend the rest of your days?

↔ ▰◆▰ ↔

If you had to live the rest of your life in a place that you have never lived in before, where would you live?

If you could keep only one article of clothing you currently own and the rest were to be thrown out, what would you keep?

↔ ▰◆▰ ↔

If you had to lose one of your five senses, which would you give up?

If you were to have one famous person alive or from history stranded with you on an island forevermore, who would you want it to be?

— ⚹ —

If you could kill the pet of anybody you know, whose pet would it be?

— ⚹ —

If you were to be recognized by posterity for one thing, what would you like to be known for?

— ⚹ —

If you could have said one sentence to Hitler while he was alive, what would you have said?

15

If you had to choose the color that describes you most accurately, which color would it be?

━━ ═◆═ ━━

If you had to convert to a different religion, which would you choose?

━━ ═◆═ ━━

If you were to drown in a liquid other than water, what would you want it to be?

━━ ═◆═ ━━

If you could reverse one sports call in history, which one would it be?

16

If you had to name the most terrifying moment of your life so far, what would it be?

If you had to be homeless for one year, where would you want to be?

If you could have one street or square or park in any city or town renamed after you, which one would you select and exactly what would the name be?

If you could be guaranteed one thing in life besides money, what would you ask for?

If you could have one person alive today call you for advice, who would you want it to be?

If you could have any person from any time in history call you for advice, and they were to listen to what you told them, who would you want to hear from?

If you could easily visit one known planet, which one would you go to?

If you could have been the author of any single book already written, which book would you want to have penned?

18

If you could have any one specific power over other people, what would it be?

If you had to lose everyone you know in a tragic accident except one person, who would you choose to survive?

If you could have one meal from your past exactly as it was, which would you repeat?

If you could become famous for doing something that you don't currently do, what would it be?

19

If you could only keep one of your five senses, which would you save?

If you could have lived during one period of time in past history, when and where would it be?

If one by one, you had to place each of the people with you right now in another period of history that you think suits them best, when and where would you place them?

If you had to describe the saddest thing that ever happened to you, what would you talk about?

20

If you had to spend one year alone in the wilderness, where would you go?

⚊⊷⚌⊶⚊

If you had to work in one type of factory for the remainder of your days but could choose which kind, what would you pick?

If you could possess one supernatural ability, what would it be?

⚊⊷⚌⊶⚊

If you had to paint your entire home, inside and out, a single color other than white, what color would you pick?

If you could have any single writer from history write your biography, who would it be?

———— ✵ ————

If you could have one current writer write your biography, who would you pick?

———— ✵ ————

If you could forever eliminate one specific type of prejudice from the earth, which would it be?

———— ✵ ————

If you could transport everyone you are with at this moment to another place, where would you all go?

22

If your home were to be totally destroyed by fire but you could save just one thing, what would it be?

· ·▰◆▰· ·

If you were to have your friends, in private, attribute a single quality to you, what would you want it to be?

· ·▰◆▰· ·

If you had to kill someone you know, who would it be, and how would you do it?

If a photograph of one part of your body were to be used in an advertisement, which part would you want to be used, and for what product or service?

If you could bring back any past leader of your country to run the country again, who would you want?

———— ✠ ————

If you could own any building in existence, which would you pick?

———— ✠ ————

If you could choose exactly what you will eat and drink for your last meal before death, what would the menu consist of?

If you could own any one existing sculpture from anywhere in the world, but not the right to ever sell it, which one would you want?

24

If you could make a gift of one thing to any single person alive today, who would it be, what would you give them, and how would you present it to them?

＋＋≡◆≡＋＋

If you could have composed any single piece of music that already exists, which would you choose?

＋＋≡◆≡＋＋

If you were invited to join one current musical group, which group would you want to be a member of, and what instrument would you play?

＋＋≡◆≡＋＋

If you were to receive any existing public award, what award would you like to win?

25

If you could decide how to spend your last day alive, what would you do?

━ ━ ━◆━ ━ ━

If you could decide what will be written on your gravestone, what would you have inscribed?

━ ━ ━◆━ ━ ━

If you had to choose the single most valuable thing you ever learned, what would it be?

━ ━ ━◆━ ━ ━

If you were kidnapped and allowed to telephone one person for one minute only, who would you call?

If you could enact one law in your country that does not currently exist, what would it be?

—— ≈❖≈ ——

If you could own only one thing for the rest of your life, what would you choose?

If you could be the current world champion in any one sport, which sport would it be?

—— ≈❖≈ ——

If you could spend a weekend in any hotel in the world with all expenses paid, which hotel would you choose?

If you could cast an actor now alive to play you in a new film, what kind of film would it be and who would you choose?

If an actor no longer alive were to play you in a film, who would you cast in the role?

If you could have your portrait painted by any painter in history, to whom would you give the commission?

If you were given one hour to spend an unlimited amount of money in any store in the world, where would it be?

If you could say one sentence to the leader of the country you are presently in, what would you say?

---- ≡◆≡ ----

If you had to choose the best advertising campaign ever created, which one would it be?

---- ≡◆≡ ----

If you could have been any person from history, who would you want to have been?

---- ≡◆≡ ----

If you could have a song written about you, what musician would you want to compose it, who would perform it, and what would it be called?

29

If you had to donate everything you own to a charity that you have never given to previously, which charity would you give to?

—— ✠ ——

If you could work for any person in the world, who would it be, and what job would you want?

—— ✠ ——

If you could discover one item that belonged to someone in history, whose would it be, and what would it be?

—— ✠ ——

If you could "uninvent" one thing in the world so that it would no longer exist, what would you choose?

30

If you were to be executed tomorrow but could decide the method, how would you prefer to go?

If you could play any position on your favorite sports team, what would it be?

If you could have a year any place in the world, all expenses paid, where would you go?

If you could see only one movie ever again, what film would you choose?

If you had to choose the title of your autobiography, what would it be?

If you could have only one piece of furniture in your house, what would you want it to be?

If you could have changed one thing about your first sexual experience, what would it be?

If you had to sleep with two famous people simultaneously, who would you choose?

If you could destroy a single tape or CD that your mate plays, what would it be?

＋－－■◆■－＋

If you could read the private diary of someone you know personally, whose diary would you read?

＋－－■◆■－＋

If you could read the diary of one person you don't know personally, whose would it be?

＋－－■◆■－＋

If you were on trial and someone you know (who is not a lawyer) had to act as your legal representative, who would you want to defend you?

33

If you could change one of your personality traits, what would it be?

If you could adopt one personality trait from someone you know, what would you take, and from whom?

If you could have a romance with any fictional character, who would it be?

If you could have one person you know be your slave for one month, who would you choose?

34

If you could have avoided living one year from your past, which year would you like to have eliminated?

＋＋≡◆≡＋＋

If you could have the home phone number of anyone in the world, whose would it be, and what would you say to them?

If you could commit one crime without being caught, what crime would you commit?

＋＋≡◆≡＋＋

If you were kidnapped and could bring along only one personal possession, what would you take?

35

If you could be the parent of one famous person, who would you want it to be?

---- ≕◆≍ ----

If you could ensure that your children never have one experience that you have had, what would it be?

---- ≕◆≍ ----

If you could eat one food in any quantity for the rest of your life with no ill affects whatsoever, what food would you choose?

If you had to eliminate one season permanently (spring, summer, autumn, or winter), which one would go?

36

If you were going to initiate a new charity, what would be its mission and who would it benefit?

If you could have been vice-president to any American president, which president would you choose?

If you could "unknow" one thing you know, what would it be?

If you could have one entire country "depopulated" as your private property, which country would you take as your own?

If you could have a secret camera in any one room in the world, what room would you put it in?

⚒◆⚒

If you had to lose one of your limbs, which one would you sacrifice?

⚒◆⚒

If you could only keep one of your limbs, which would you choose to keep?

⚒◆⚒

If you were to have sex with two people simultaneously that you have known from your own past, who would you pick?

38

If you were to be the personal valet of any one man or woman from history, who would you want to work for?

If you could hire any architect alive or from history to design your dream house, who would you pick, and where would you build it?

If you could have invented anything from history, what would you pick?

If you could invent something that currently does not exist, what would it be?

39

If you could have been the first person to discover any part of the world, what place would you want to have found?

If you could have any music group alive today play at your birthday party, which group would you hire?

＋＋　≡◆≡　＋＋

If you could have any music group that no longer exists play at your birthday party, who would you want?

＋＋　≡◆≡　＋＋

If you could have a secret hideaway to escape to with a lover, where would it be?

40

If you were to cast the two romantic leads of a new film with any actors alive, who would you pick?

If you could choose the way you will die, how would you want it to happen?

If you could foresee a single day of your future in its entirety, what date would you select?

If you had to have fought in any war in history, which would you have fought in?

If you could ask God any single question, what would it be?

If you could be one article of clothing, what would you be, and who would you want to belong to?

If you had to be someone's body part, what would you be, and on whose body?

If you were to be rescued from a desert island, by whom would you want to be rescued?

42

If you had to eat the same meal for the rest of your life, morning, noon, and night, without worrying about nutrition, what would you eat?

If you could live the life of any fictional character, which character would it be?

If you could have been any past president of the United States, who would you have been?

If you could have one person from history work for you as your personal assistant, who would it be?

43

If you could have the mind of someone you know but remain in your own body, whose brain would you take?

If you could have the mind of someone from history and remain in your own body, whose would you choose?

If you could coach any current sports team professionally, which would you choose?

If you had to name the single most regrettable thing about your country's history, what would it be?

If you could star in a love scene with any living actor, who would you want to act with, and where would you want it filmed?

—+— ≣◊≣ —+—

If you could have survived any historic disaster, which would you choose?

—+— ≣◊≣ —+—

If you could discover that something you thought was true was actually false, what would you wish it to be?

—+— ≣◊≣ —+—

If you could leave flowers on any one person's grave every week whether you knew them or not, who would it be?

45

If you could be invisible for one hour, where would you go and what would you do?

If you could relive one romantic date from high school just as it was, which would it be?

If you could relive one romantic date from high school as you would like it to have been, which would you choose?

If you had to give up all sexual activity for one year, how much money would you demand (minimum) in return?

46

If you had to keep one part of your mate's body permanently in the freezer, what part would you save?

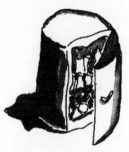

If you were the sole survivor of a plane crash with everyone present and had to choose someone to eat in order to survive, who would you select?

If you could eliminate one hereditary characteristic from your family, what would it be?

If you could be a student of any university in the world right now, where would you enroll?

If you could host a dinner party in any room in the world (without having to clean up), where would you want to have it?

If you could host a dinner party inviting any four people from history, who would you invite and where would the party take place?

If you were to be married to someone who is famous now, who would you pick to be your new spouse?

If you had to be married to someone famous from the past who is no longer alive, who would you like it to be?

If you had to have sex with someone that you know personally who is not of your sexually preferred gender, who would you select?

If you could arrange a rock concert with any three musicians or groups to play on the same bill, who would you invite?

If you could relive one single day from your past exactly as it was the first time, what day would you choose to experience all over again?

If you could wake up tomorrow to learn that the major newspaper headlines were about you, what would you want them to say?

If you could eliminate one day from your past so that you had never had to live through it, which day would you erase?

— ⊫◆⊨ —

If you could go back in time, as yourself, to live for one year at any point in history, what year would you choose, and where would you go?

— ⊫◆⊨ —

If you could have had one composer from history write a symphony for you, who would it be?

— ⊫◆⊨ —

If you were to receive a letter today from anyone you have known during your lifetime, who would it be from and what would it say?

50

If you could have a telegram from one famous person now alive, who would it be from, and what would it say?

━━◆━━

If you could have a telegram from one person from history, who would it be from and what would it say?

If one part of your body was to become a religious relic, which part would you like it to be?

━━◆━━

If you were to be successful in another profession, what would you want to do?

If you could have been the architect of any one building in history, which building would you choose?

If you could have directed any film in history, what movie would it be?

— ≈◆≋ —

If you had to spend all of your vacations for the rest of your life in the same place, where would you go?

— ≈◆≋ —

If you were stranded on a desert island and could have with you only one object you currently own, what would you take?

52

If you won a lottery, what is the first thing you would do?

If you could have a secret listening device in any one room in the world, which room would you like it to be in?

If you had to inhabit the body of someone you know personally while keeping your own mind, whose body would you take?

If you could be a member of any club or association in the world, what would it be?

53

If you were given $5,000 to spend in one store in the world, where would you do your shopping?

If you could steal one thing in the world, other than money, without getting caught, what would you take?

If you could be the lover of any person alive other than your current lover, who would you pick?

If you could have been a lover of any person in history, who would you choose?

54

If you had to die in one of history's disasters, which one would you pick?

If you could take revenge on any person you have ever known, who would it be, why do they deserve it, and how would you do it?

If you were to perform in the circus, what would you do?

If you could master one type of cuisine, which one would you choose?

If you could be master chef in any restaurant in the world, where would you choose to cook?

If you could ensure that your child has one experience that you have had yourself, what would you want it to be?

＋ ✦ ＋

If you could have a free telephone line to any one person in the world, who would it be?

＋ ✦ ＋

If you could retract one lie you have told in your life, which would it be?

If you were stranded on a desert island and could have only one piece of music to listen to, what would it be?

--- ≡◆≡ ---

If you were to die in a public place, exactly what spot would you choose?

--- ≡◆≡ ---

If you were elected to be leader of a foreign country tomorrow, what country would you want it to be and what would be your first official act?

--- ≡◆≡ ---

If you had to have one piece of music softly playing in your mind for the rest of your life, what would you want it to be?

57

If you had to have one family member (besides your spouse) witness your next sexual act, who would you pick?

----- ≡◆≡ -----

If you could see anyone alive fully naked, who would you select?

----- ≡◆≡ -----

If you could see one famous person from history fully naked, who would it be?

----- ≡◆≡ -----

If you could be any sports figure now alive, who would you want to be?

If you were to give one person you know an award for something, who would it be, and for what?

――――✕✦✕――――

If you had to choose someone with you right now to be president of the United States, who would you want it to be?

――――✕✦✕――――

If you could become rich doing one thing that you currently don't do, what would you want it to be?

If you were to be a machine, what machine would you be?

59

If you could erase any one murder from history, which would it be?

＋━ ▰◆▱ ━＋

If you had to change citizenship, which country would you want to become a citizen of?

＋━ ▰◆▱ ━＋

If you could be married anywhere in the world, where would the wedding take place?

If you could be buried anywhere, where would it be?

60

If you could ensure one single personality trait in your children, what would you want it to be?

━━◆━━

If you could run any single company, institution, or organization in the world, which would you choose?

━━◆━━

If you had to select any single manmade object that best represents your personality, what would it be?

━━◆━━

If you could gain total memory of one year of your life so far, which year would you pick?

If you could overthrow any government in the world, which one would you replace?

·—·— ≡✦≡ —·—·

If you were to have a one-night stand with a current world leader, who would you choose?

·—·— ≡✦≡ —·—·

If you were to bear the child of a famous person alive today, whose child would you like to have?

·—·— ≡✦≡ —·—·

If you could have borne the child of a famous person no longer living, who would you choose?

62

If you could choose any historic figure to read your eulogy, who would you want to do it?

If you could call any person from history for advice tonight, who would you prefer to talk to?

If you could put anyone in prison, who would you lock up?

If you could undo one sexual encounter in your life so that it never happened, which one would it be?

If you could choose the music at your own funeral, what would it be, and who would play it?

If you had to sleep with someone you despise in exchange for one thing, what is it that you would demand?

If you had to spy on your own country for another country, which nation would you do it for?

If you had to name your single worst fear, what would it be?

If you had to describe the single worst thing a friend could do to you, what would it be?

If you were to invent an award to give to one commercial company, which one would you award, and for what?

If you could resolve any single dispute, anywhere in the world, what would you solve?

If you could be a contestant on any game show, which would you like to be on?

If you could read the mind of anyone you know, who would it be?

If you could read the mind of someone famous, who would it be?

If you could dance any one dance perfectly, which dance would you choose?

If you could be the editor of any single magazine, what publication would you pick?

If you were elected to be the leader of the United States tomorrow, what would be your first act?

<hr />

If you could eliminate one thing you do each day in the bathroom so that you never had to do it again, what would it be?

If you had to have your mate get a part of their body pierced, exactly where would you want it to be?

<hr />

If you could only hear one voice that you are familiar with for the rest of your life from the mouth of all people, whose would it be?

67

If you could serve in one capacity in the military (in which you haven't already served), what would you want to do?

⚊⚊ ⚏⚎⚏ ⚊⚊

If you could eliminate forevermore one cause of death on earth, what would it be?

If you had to choose the best book in history, which book would get the prize?

⚊⚊ ⚏⚎⚏ ⚊⚊

If you had to choose the worst book ever written, what would it be?

68

If you could use only one cosmetic item for the rest of your life, what would you choose?

If you could cure any disease, which would it be?

If you could be the owner of any current team in professional sports, which one would you want?

If you had to eliminate one odor from the earth, which one would you get rid of?

If you had to permanently give up your children to the care of someone you know, who would you wish it to be?

If you had to give up your children to the care of someone famous, who would you pick?

If you were to select a food that best describes your character, what food would it be?

If you could arrange a jam session with any three musicians in history, who would you include?

70

If you could invent one new home appliance, what would it do?

If you were to be someone's personal computer, whose would you like to be?

If you were to be a news correspondent posted to any foreign country, where would you like to go?

If you had to choose a time in history when overall things were worse than any other single time, when would you say it was?

71

If you could take away the vocal chords of any person, who would it be?

If you had to have one platonic friend witness your next sexual act, who would you ask?

If you could be a guest on any television talk show, which would it be?

If you were suddenly naked in front of everyone at work, what would you say to them?

If you could keep only one thing that is in your bathroom right now, as the only thing in there forever, what would you save?

— ≡◆≡ —

If you could have prevented one event in history, what event would you eliminate?

— ≡◆≡ —

If you had to rename your hometown, what would you call it?

— ≡◆≡ —

If you could teach your children only one lesson in life, what would it be?

73

If you had to be a member of another family you know, which family would you join?

———✦———

If you had to cast living actors to play each of the people with you right now in a new film, who would you choose to play each person?

———✦———

If you had to choose the worst work of art ever created, what would you choose?

———✦———

If you had to choose the greatest work of art in history, what would you say is the best?

74

If you had the chance to make one purchase that you have passed up in your lifetime, what would it be?

If you had to describe your idea of the perfect mate, how would you do it?

If you could have been the producer of any single television show or series, which one would you pick?

If you could own any single newspaper in the world, which one would you pick?

If you could choose any six people to be the pallbearers at your funeral, who would you choose?

· · ·

If you had to repeat your exact life over again exactly as it was, from any age, what age would you go back to?

If you could find one thing, besides money, in your family attic, what would you want to discover?

· · ·

If you could go back to any age and start a different life, what age would that be?

If you had to eliminate a single art form from the earth henceforth and forevermore, which one would you get rid of?

--- ✦ ---

If you had to name the single most important quality of a good mate, what would it be?

--- ✦ ---

If the world could henceforth have only one single art form, what do you think it should be?

--- ✦ ---

If you had been the original designer of one existing corporate logo, which one would you select?

If you could wear only one color, besides white or black, for the rest of your life, what would you wear?

—— ⟐ ——

If you had to eat in only one restaurant for the rest of your life, which one would you choose?

—— ⟐ ——

If you had to be represented by an object in your home, what would you choose?

—— ⟐ ——

If you could have changed any one thing about the death of one of your relatives, what would you alter?

If you had been the reporter to have broken one news event during your lifetime, what would you like it to have been?

If you could have any type of fresh cut flowers delivered to your home every week, what one type would you pick?

If you had to be the underwear of someone famous, who would you choose to wear you?

If you could have refereed one sports match in history, which one would you pick?

If you could put a new tattoo on someone you know, who would you pick, what would it be, and where would you put it?

If you could make someone else live one moment from your own life, who would you select, and what moment?

If you could keep only one home appliance, which would you keep?

If you were to be reincarnated as an animal, what kind would you want to be?

80

If you could ask a single question of a dead relative, what would it be and of whom would you ask it?

If you could have changed one thing about your parents while you were a child, what would it have been?

If you had to have a personal friend redecorate your house, who would you pick to do it?

If you could give a single piece of advice to the film industry in Hollywood, what would you say?

81

If you had to rename each of the people you are with right now, what would you call each of them?

··— ≡◈≡ —··

If you had to marry someone that you presently know unromantically, and spend the rest of your life as their spouse, who would you choose?

··— ≡◈≡ —··

If you had to choose one country in the world other than the United States to become the only superpower of the twenty-first century, which country would you pick?

··— ≡◈≡ —··

If you had to choose one person currently in the U.S. government to control the nuclear forces instead of the president, who would it be?

If you could choose both major candidates for the next United States presidential race, what two people would you pick?

———— ≡◆≡ ————

If you could have worked for anyone in history, in your own field, who would you choose?

———— ≡◆≡ ————

If you could have been the person who discovered any country in history, which country would you like to have been the first to find?

If you had to cancel one hour of the day, every day, which hour would you eliminate?

If you could go back in time, as yourself, to observe any single event from history, what would you want to witness?

If you were to choose a musical instrument that best describes your character, what would it be?

If you had to exchange one physical attribute with someone in the room, who would you pick, and what would you exchange with them?

If you had to cancel one month of the year forevermore, so that period of time no longer existed, which month would go?

If you could choose one new symbol for your family crest, what would it be?

If you could do any job in the world for one day, what would it be?

If you could be anywhere in history for one day, as someone famous from that time, where would you like to be, when, and as who?

If you had to choose the best television show ever made, which one would you pick?

If you could have been any sports figure from history, who would you want to have been?

If you could change one thing about your life, what would it be?

If you had to choose the prize for the best movie in history, what film would win?

If you had to pick the worst movie in history, which one would get the dubious honor?

86

If you could practice only one of the principle vices henceforth, which one would you stick with?

——— ⋈ ———

If you could have discovered one medical cure in history, which one would you choose?

If you could have sued any one person in your life, who would it be, and for what?

——— ⋈ ———

If you could have been a jury member in any court case in history, which trial would you choose?

If you had to murder someone, how would you do it?

If you had to commit suicide by jumping from a tall height, where would you do it?

If you could choose the very last thing you will see before death, what would it be?

If you had to trade houses with someone you know, who would it be?

If you had to have been any dictator or tyrant in history, which one would you choose to have been?

----※◆※----

If you could add one sentence to the U.S. Constitution, what would it say?

----※◆※----

If you could bomb one building in the world without hurting any people, which would you blow up?

----※◆※----

If you could be the author of any one quotation from history, what words would you like to have uttered?

89

If you had to confess to one crime you have already committed, what would you confess to?

If you could choose, from what you own right now, what clothes to be buried in when you die, what would you wear?

If you had to describe the worst job interview in your life, what job would it have been for?

If you could have hit any homerun in baseball history, which one would you choose?

If you were to be any famous person's personal masseuse, whose would you like to be?

———✥———

If you could give anonymous advice to any one person about their appearance, who would it be, and what would you say?

———✥———

If you could be on the cover of any magazine next month, which magazine would you want it to be, and what would the caption say?

If you had to pick the worst meal you've ever eaten, what would it be?

If everything in the world had to have the same odor, what scent would you want it to be?

If you could give your parents one gift, what would you give them?

If you were to receive one honorary degree in your lifetime, which university would you prefer, and for what accomplishment?

If you could have given one speech in history, which one would you pick?

If you could have been on the United States Supreme Court for any single case in its history, which would you select?

If you could physically strike one person from your past (that you didn't), who would you hit, and where?

If you could change one election result from the past so that the loser had won, which one would it be?

If you had to die from something other than old age, how would you prefer to go?

If you had to name the worst job in the world, what would it be?

———— ✠ ————

If you could own the entire wardrobe of any one television character, from the show they're on, whose clothes would you want?

———— ✠ ————

If you could cancel one vacation you have taken, lose all memory of it, and get your money back, what vacation would you choose?

———— ✠ ————

If you had to choose the worst work experience you've ever had, what would you pick?

94

If you could cancel forever a single thing you have to do every day other than your job, what would it be?

If you had to go tonight to be tattooed, where on your body would you have it done and what image would you select?

If you could realize a dream that you have had while asleep, what dream would you pick?

If you could choose only one color and image for your country's new flag, what would it look like?

If you had to identify the worst hotel room you have ever stayed in, where was it?

If you had to name the most important invention in history, what would win?

If you had to describe the best kiss you've ever had, how would you describe it?

If your house were to be haunted by the ghost of one person from history, who would you wish it to be?

If you had to choose the best song ever composed, which one would it be?

· · ✦ · ·

If you had to choose the worst song ever composed, which one would you pick?

· · ✦ · ·

If you had to change your race, what would you want to be?

· · ✦ · ·

If you had to select the most beautiful face in history, whose face would you pick?

97

If you had to pick the worst sexual experience of your life, what would it be?

—◄•►—

If you could solve one unsolved crime, which one would you solve?

—◄•►—

If you were to be renamed after someone from history, whose name would you want?

—◄•►—

If you could accomplish only one thing in the rest of your life, what would it be?

98

If you could have the sex life of any person from history, but remain yourself, who would you choose?

— ≡◆≡ —

If you could have anyone's eyes in the world, whose eyes would you want?

If you could completely eliminate one of your pet peeves, what would you get rid of?

— ≡◆≡ —

If you could win any competition in the world, what would it be for?

If you had to choose the worst telephone call you've ever had, what call was it?

If you had to choose the best telephone call you've ever had, which was it?

＋－ ≡◆≡ ＋－

If you could have the hair of someone you know, whose would you take?

＋－ ≡◆≡ ＋－

If you had to serve a life sentence in jail for one crime, what crime would you commit?

100

If you just learned that you had exactly one year to live, what would you do with your remaining time?

If you were to have only one of the prime virtues, which one would you want to possess?

If you could break one current world sports record, which one would it be?

If you had to recall the worst date you've ever been on, which one was it?

If you were to permanently give up sex for one thing other than money, what would you do it for?

If you could tell your boss one thing with complete impunity, what would you say?

If you could have prevented one natural disaster that actually happened, what would it be?

If you could hold one position in current government, what would you want to do?

102

If your plane was about to crash and you had time to write one quick note, to whom would you write, and what would you say?

If you were to adopt an orphan from another country, which country would the child come from?

If you were to pick a moment in history when, all things considered, the world was better off, which would it be?

If you could change one thing to make life easier for your own gender, what would you change?

If you were allowed to eat only one vegetable for the rest of your life, which one would it be?

If you could change the ending of any book ever written, which one would you pick and how would you change it?

If you had to spend one weekend alone in a single store but could remove nothing, which store would you pick?

If you could referee or judge one sport as a permanent job, which would you choose?

If you could give a single piece of advice to the automobile industry, what would you tell them?

If you had to choose someone to sleep with your mate, who would you pick?

If you had to sacrifice your own life for one thing, what would it be?

If you had to repeat one alcohol or drug experience you've had, which one would you relive?

105

If you could see through the clothes of any one person at all times, who would it be?

If you could call any living person to ask for advice tonight, who would you call?

If you could recover one thing you've lost in your lifetime, what would you wish to find?

If you could memorize one book from history in its entirety, which book would you want it to be?

If you could make a sequel to any movie you have ever seen, which one would it be?

If you were given a yacht today, what would you name it?

If you were given a racehorse, what would you name it?

If you had to name the best purchase you've ever made, which one would you choose?

If you could spend one year looking for one thing in the world, what would you search for?

If you had written one song from this century yourself, which would you like to have written?

If you could have been told one thing that you weren't told when you were a teenager, what would you like to have heard?

If you were sentenced to spend the rest of your life in a prison cell with one person you know, who would you take?

If you could pick one famous person to be your neighbor, who would you have next door to you?

··—··✦··—··

If you could live on any one street in the world, which address would you choose?

··—··✦··—··

If you could sing any one song beautifully and perfectly, which one would you pick?

··—··✦··—··

If you were going to turn to crime to support yourself from now on, what kind of criminal would you become?

If you could occupy the world described in a novel, which would you choose?

If you could change one thing about your home, what would you make different?

If you could make one fairytale or fable come true with yourself in it, which would you pick?

If you could teach a person any single thing, who and what would you choose?

110

If you had to cancel one day of the week forever, which day would go?

If you could break one world's record for anything other than sports, what would it be?

If you had to choose the worst home you've ever lived in, which one was it?

If you could be the only one to hear the confession of one criminal from history, who would it be?

111

If you had to choose the most important single event of this century, what would win the honor?

If you could leave a time capsule the size of a microwave oven to be found centuries from now, what would you put inside it?

If you were asked what to put in a new breakfast cereal box as a gimmick, what would you pick?

If you had to secretly dispose of a dead body, how would you do it?

112

If you could be forgiven for one thing in your life, what would you choose?

If you had to predict the most important development of the twenty-first century, what do you think it will be?

If you could only have sex once more in your life, when would you do it, with whom, and where?

If you could romantically kiss someone that you never have, who would you want it to be?

113

If you could keep your mate but have the rest of the world populated by only one gender, which would it be?

＊＋≡＋≡＋＋

If you could have a voodoo doll that functioned for one person you know, who would that person be, and what would you use it for?

＊＋≡＋≡＋＋

If you could change one thing about your city or town or neighborhood, what would you alter?

＊＋≡＋≡＋＋

If you could firebomb any store or business, which would you do it to?

114

If you had to pick the most important quality for a leader of your country, what would it be?

If you could change the ending to one movie you have seen, which one would it be, and how would you reshoot it?

If you could reverse the effects of any one environmental problem that we are currently faced with, what problem would you choose to mend?

If you could, in retrospect, have purchased a large quantity of stock the day it was first issued, which one would it have been?

If you had to choose the single biggest mistake you have made in life so far, what would it be?

If you could throw a party in any existing interior space in the world, where would you have it?

If you could arrange for any two singers to record a duet together, which two would you pick, and what song would you have them sing?

If you had to describe your worst medical experience, what would it be?

If you could give anonymous advice to one set of parents you know about how they are raising their kids, who would it be and what would you tell them?

If you could go back in time just long enough to tell the founding fathers of America one thing, what would you tell or warn them of?

If you could eliminate one habit your mate has, what would you have them stop doing?

If you had to spend one weekend alone in a single public building or institution, which building would you choose?

117

If you could have one current politician removed from office, who would you get rid of?

—————

If you had to name one thing that your mate could do to assure that you would leave them forever, what would it be?

—————

If you could eliminate one habit you have, what would you stop doing?

—————

If you just learned that you were to die in exactly one hour, what would you do?

118

If you had to drop a nuclear bomb on one country, where would you drop it?

❈

If you could have witnessed any biblical event, what would you want to have seen?

❈

If you could work for any corporation for which you don't currently work, which would you choose?

❈

If your own ashes were to be kept in an urn, after you die, where would you want the urn kept?

If you could plan the perfect evening out, what would it involve?

If you could program the perfect evening of television shows, which ones would you select, and in what order?

If you had to kill one person you work with, who would you off?

If you had to name the dumbest purchase you've ever made, which would it be?

120

If you could receive all the products from a single company for free (but could not resell them), which company would you choose?

If you had to name the one thing that makes you angriest about a relative, what would it be?

If you were to become the sex slave of one person from history, who would you want it to be?

If you had to describe the perfect body, what would you say about it?

If you could have the autograph of one person from history, who would it be?

If you could have any view from your home, what would it be of?

If you could have asked Richard Nixon one thing, what would you have asked?

If you could have the world's largest collection of one thing, what would it be?

122

If you could have been the hero from any war, which war would it be, and for what heroic deed?

If you were to inhabit the world of any video or computer game, which one would you select?

If you could leave only one existing book for the world to have five hundred years from now (other than this one), which book would you leave?

If you just learned that tomorrow morning you were to be permanently exiled from your country and could take just three things with you, what would they be?

If you could teach your pet to do one thing, what would it be?

If you could teach your mate to do one thing, what would it be?

If you could write letters to only one person for the rest of your life, who would receive them?

If you were to be reincarnated as someone you know, who would it be?

If you were to be given an acting role in a current TV show, who would you want to play?

If you could arrange for one thing to befall your boss, what would you have happen?

If you could start a new rock band, what would you name it?

If you could have a servant come to your house every day for one hour, what would you have them do?

125

If you were to have your portrait painted, what would you choose as the setting?

If you could choose the very last thing you would see before you die, what would it be?

If you were to be cremated, where would you want your ashes scattered?

If you had to choose your best sexual experience, what would it be?

126

If you could, it retrospect, thank one teacher you had in school for what they taught you, who would it be, and what would you thank them for?

If you had to pick the worst television series ever made, what would win?

If you could reverse the ongoing extinction of any animal now endangered, which animal would you choose to save?

If you could make a film from any book never produced as a film, what book would you pick?

127

If you could change one thing to make life easier for your children, what would you do?

———— ◆ ————

If you had to sell your soul for one thing, what would it be?

———— ◆ ————

If you could achieve absolute success in only one area of your life, what would you want it to be?

———— ◆ ————

If you could determine the careers of your children, what would you have them do, assuming they would be successful at it?

128

If you could visit only one more place in the world that you have never been, where would you go for this final voyage?

If you could have anyone locked in a room so that you could torment them for a day, who would you choose, and how would you torment them?

If you had to pick the most difficult question you could be asked, what would it be?

If you could have the answer to any question, what would you ask?

129

If²...

(500 More Questions for the Game of Life)

The human imagination is infinite. The fantasies it creates thrill us and uplift us. They even help us to find our way in life. This second collection of "If . . ." questions picks up where its predecessor left off . . . somewhere deep in the extraordinary territory of what people hope for, dream for, and value about each other and themselves.

There is one immediate purpose of these 500 queries: to provoke the mind. Some are humorous, some more serious, and some even quite difficult to answer. Once you begin to play, you may find laughter, tears, revelation, learning, surprise, or contemplation. But you will never lack the potential for fascinating discussions.

As well as the "classic" topics (sex, money, children, death), *If²* . . . includes queries related to issues on the minds of people today, such as welfare, taxes, health care, the environment, and many more. Each of these alone can give rise to further discussion and other questions. Use this book to find out more about your neighbors or your friends; ask "If" questions of your teachers, use them for interviews, call in one to a radio show, send one out on the Internet. Few people can resist engaging in the discussions that "If . . ." initiates. The difficulty with thinking up and compiling these questions was that we were repeatedly interrupted by the irresistible urge to try to answer them, our own imaginations tempting us constantly from the asking, toward the answering. May you, too, give in completely to the same wonderful temptation.

If you found out for certain there is a Heaven and a Hell, how would you change your life?

If you could determine the age at which you will die, but with no guarantees regarding health or money, how old would you like to be when you go?

If you had to select the one thing in life you feel the most guilty about, what would it be?

If you could rid the earth of one thing, what would it be?

135

If you were to close down any charity, which one would you pick?

If you could have overheard a specific conversation between any two people, which would it be?

If you could have the hair of any Hollywood celebrity, whose would you want?

If you had to describe the most memorable night of your life, what would you say?

136

If you could have the power to hypnotize anyone for a day, who would you pick and what would you have them do?

···≡◆≡···

If you had to name the best album cover ever, which would it be?

···≡◆≡···

If you had to choose the one thing that gives you the most comfort, what would you say?

···≡◆≡···

If you could have witnessed one event from your family's history, what would you want to see?

If you had to choose a single vice president in the history of the United States to become president, who would you pick?

If you had to give up your favorite food forever, what is the minimum amount of money you would demand in return?

⚜

If you had to name the best live musical performance you have ever attended, which would you pick?

⚜

If you had to name the best speech or presentation you've ever heard, what would it be?

138

If you had to name the one thing that most frightens you about growing old, what would it be?

If you could be more ambitious in only one aspect of your life, what would it be?

If you could have anyone from history welcome you into the afterlife, who would you want it to be?

If you had to nominate one person you have known for sainthood, who would you choose?

139

If you were to spend the rest of your life in the company of a single type of animal, which would you choose?

If you had to constantly carry a weapon of some kind, what would it be?

✦

If you could trade your derrière for that of someone else, whose would you want?

✦

If you had to name the one most important ingredient of human beauty, what would you say it is?

140

If you had to give a prize for the most sexually attractive politician in U.S. history, who would win it?

If you had to name the single most erotic part of the human body, what would it be?

If you had to name the least erotic part of the human body, what would it be?

If you were to add a thirteenth month to the year, where would you insert it?

141

If you could rid your family of one thing, what would it be?

If you had to name the all-time best song, which would you pick?

If you could say (or have said) one thing to your father on his deathbed, what would it be?

If you could have one thing made out of pure gold, what would you choose?

If you had to pick one experience or situation when you were the most decisive, which would it be?

If you could have only one part of your body massaged every day, what part would you choose?

If you could be the character in any spy novel, who would you choose to be?

If you had to name the time when you came closest to death, when would it have been?

If you could make anyone in the world do something each day, who would it be, and what would you have them do?

━━━◆━━━

If you could reverse a single policy of the pope, what would you change?

━━━◆━━━

If you were to choose the breed you would be if you were a dog, which type would best suit you?

━━━◆━━━

If you had to name the one thing that repeatedly makes you angriest, what would it be?

If you could organize a family reunion with all of your dead relatives, where would you hold it?

If you could change one thing about the building you work in, what would you alter?

If you were to decide the legal age for sexual consent, what age would it be?

If you were to prescribe a cure for grief, what would it entail?

If someone were trying to woo your lover away from you, what methods would bring them the most success?

If you had to name the one thing you have witnessed in your life that best represents Goodness, what would you say?

If you could have modeled in one of Calvin Klein's advertising campaigns for either underwear or fragrance, which ad would you like to have been in?

If you had to name the best music album ever recorded, which would you select?

If you had to name the one time in your life when you were the most angry, when was it?

＋◆＋

If you were to be killed by an animal, what kind would you want it to be?

＋◆＋

If you were to be tied naked in bed and have your lover melt an ice cube on a single part of your body, without touching you otherwise, where would you want them to melt it?

＋◆＋

If you could change one thing about your face to make it more beautiful, what would you alter?

147

If you had to choose the one animal or insect species that is most beautiful, which would you pick?

If you could have any view in the world visible from your bed, what would it be?

If you had to name the most beautiful bed you have ever occupied, what would it be?

If you could exchange work space (e.g., office or cubicle), but not jobs, with someone you presently work with, whose spot would you take?

148

If you could have prevented any single fashion idea or trend from ever happening, which would you have stopped?

If you were to select a moment when you were convinced that an angel was watching over you, when would it have been?

If you could suddenly find out that one work of fiction was actually true, what book would you select?

If you were to have bells ring out loud automatically (for all to hear) every time you did a certain thing, what would it be?

149

If you could have a single button beside your bed that did one thing, what would you want it to do?

If you could have any single kind of appliance attached to your bed, what would it be?

✦

If you were to have Shakespeare to dinner tonight and could invite one other person from history, who would you pick?

✦

If you could have prevented one book from ever having been written, which book would it be?

If there were to be one person, among those whom you know, who could from now on read all your thoughts, who would you have it be?

If you had a spot somewhere on your body that, when touched by anyone else, instantly gave you an orgasm, where would you want it to be?

If you could have had one person in your life be less candid with you than they were (or are), who would it be?

If you could have had one person in your life be more candid with you than they were (or are), who would it be?

151

If you had to name a smell that always makes you nostalgic, what would it be?

If you could train a pet bird to do one thing for you and always return home again, what would it do?

If you could have been Judge Lance Ito, what one thing would you have done differently?

If, in order to save your life, someone you know had to donate their heart to you (without dying), whose heart would you want inside yourself?

152

If you could have heard the deathbed confession of one person from history, who would you pick?

If you were going to die in ten minutes and could confess only one thing in order to pass with peace of mind, what would you say?

If you could change places with any of your friends, who would you choose to be?

If you could ruin someone's reputation, whose would it be, and how would you do it?

If you could be the house cat or lap dog of any person on earth, whose would you choose to be?

—·—✠·✠—·—

If you could cause any single person to change their mind about one thing or on one topic, who would you pick, and how would you change their thinking?

If you could wake up tomorrow in your own bed, but in another place anywhere in the world inside or outside, where would you like it to be?

—·—✠·✠—·—

If your children could read only four books while growing up, which would you have them read?

154

If you could eliminate a single kind of danger (other than death) for your children, what would it be?

━ ✦ ━

If you were to pick a city whose character best represents your own personality, which would you choose?

━ ✦ ━

If you could prevent someone you know from overusing one word, who would it be, and what word would it be?

━ ✦ ━

If you could see the inside of any single athlete's locker, whose would it be?

If you could have X-ray vision on one person you work with, who would you want it to be?

⋯⋯⋯⋯

If you could be more candid with one person you know from now on, who would it be?

⋯⋯⋯⋯

If you could have taken better care of one thing in your life, what would it have been?

⋯⋯⋯⋯

If you could change one thing about the way you were disciplined as a child, what would you alter?

156

If you suddenly found the courage to do one thing you have always been afraid of doing, what would you want it to be?

If you had to describe your worst experience with blood, what would you say?

If you were to be the sole confessor of one person on earth, without being able to ever betray their trust no matter what they told you, who would you want it to be?

If you could choose any three songs to compile on a disc to wake up (slowly) to every morning, what would they be, and in what order?

If you could have witnessed the childhood of someone famous, whose would it be?

If you had to exchange wardrobes with someone you know, whose clothes would you want?

If you could have won a single thing you tried for in your lifetime but didn't win, what would it be?

If you had to name your greatest conquest in life thus far, what would it be?

158

If you could keep only one book you currently own, which would you choose?

If you could have a set of bed sheets made of anything in the world, what material would you choose?

If you could have known someone as a child that you now know, who would it be?

If you had to name the worst song to wake up to in the morning, what would it be?

If you could commission any living author to write a new book, who would you choose, and what would you have them write about?

— ≡♦≡ —

If you could have had your mind changed on one issue or decision in your lifetime, what would it have been?

— ≡♦≡ —

If you could have changed the mind of one person from history on one issue, who and what issue would you pick?

— ≡♦≡ —

If someone you work with could have X-ray vision on you, who would you most hate it to be?

160

If you were to start an orphanage for children anywhere in the world, where would you want it to be?

If you had to choose the single most charming person you have ever met, who would win?

If just one aspect of your life functioned perfectly forevermore, what would you pick?

If you had to pay one dollar for every time you thought of sex in any form, how long would it be before you went bankrupt?

If you could change one thing about the American electoral system, what would it be?

***

If you could solve one world problem by pledging your own permanent celibacy, what would you do it for?

***

If you could eliminate one thing other people's children do, what would it be?

***

If you had to name the most dangerous thing you have ever done on purpose, what would it be?

162

If you came home to find your teenage son or daughter in bed with a postal delivery person, what would you say to them in one sentence?

If you were to be paid to write a new book on any subject you wished, what would it be about?

If you had to eat the cooking of one person you know personally for the rest of your life, whose would you want it to be?

If you were to have three new baby daughters, what would you name them?

If you could give hair back to any balding person you know, who would you pick?

———— ⌖ ————

If you found out that there is no afterlife in any sense, how would you change your life?

If you had to name the one thing that really makes your day, what would it be?

———— ⌖ ————

If you had to name the one thing that can most readily ruin your day, what would it be?

164

If you could change one thing about your country's history, what would you alter?

———

If you could change one nonphysical thing about your spouse or lover, what would it be?

———

If you had to eliminate one emotion from your life, which would it be?

———

If you could suddenly be irresistibly charming for one day only, what would you do?

165

If you could give a bronze cast of one part of your body to your most recent ex, what part would it be?

＊ ━＋≡ ＋━

If you had to identify the one thing destiny probably held in store for you, what would you say it is?

＊ ━＋≡ ＋━

If you could change one thing about your typical day, what would it be?

＊ ━＋≡ ＋━

If you discovered a Shakespeare manuscript that no one else had ever seen, what would you do with it?

166

If you could be right behind any single person in line at the Gates of Heaven, who would you choose?

---- ≡♦≡ ----

If you found yourself at the Pearly Gates and had one chance to make your case for entry, what would you say?

---- ≡♦≡ ----

If you had to name your greatest accomplishment so far in life, what would you say it was?

If you could have back one article of clothing you gave or threw away, what would you want it to be?

If you were to name something that your parents or spouse should have felt guilty about but didn't, what would it be?

If you had to name the most gullible person you know, who is it?

If you could stop loving someone, who would it be?

If you suddenly found yourself at work, wearing women's erotic underwear and nothing else, what would you say (in one sentence) to your fellow workers?

168

If you could enact one law related to royal marriages, what would it say?

If you could give one thing to each of your ex-lovers, what would you give them?

+—+ ≡◆≡ +—+

If you had to name the person who turned out to be furthest from your first impression of them, who would it be?

+—+ ≡◆≡ +—+

If you were to name the most clear proof that evil exists in the world, what would you say?

If you could drink only one type of alcoholic drink for the rest of your life, what would you choose?

If you had to fight a duel tomorrow at dawn, and you could determine the type of weapons you both would use, what would they be?

If you could have the vocabulary of any person you know, who would you pick?

If you had to leave everything you own to your alma mater, but you could specify what it would be used for, what would you request?

170

If you were to name the best "I told you so" you ever got to deliver, what was it?

⊷ ⊷ ⊷

If you were to pick the one thing that always makes you smile, what would it be?

⊷ ⊷ ⊷

If you had to choose the celebrity you most resemble in personality, who would it be?

⊷ ⊷ ⊷

If you were to have two new baby sons, what would you name them?

171

If you had to confess to the most evil thing you have ever done, what would it be?

If you had to name one advantage daughters have over sons, what would you say it is?

If you could cause something that happened in the history of the world to happen again in order to teach something to those in the present, what would you have re-happen?

If you could change places with any celebrity in the world, but would have to remain that person forever, who would you be?

172

If you had to name the nicest thing that has ever happened to you completely by chance, what would it be?

If you were to confess to how many people you have honestly been in love with, what would you say?

If you wanted your death to have the maximum dramatic effect on people who knew you, how would you choose to die?

If you had to give the same gift to everyone you know next Christmas, what would it be?

If you could touch any single person in the world with only the tip of your index finger, who would you pick, and where would you touch them?

If you had to receive the same (affordable) gift, besides money, from everyone you know on your next birthday, what would you want?

If, in retrospect, you could have been nicer to one person in your life, who would it be?

If you could stop overusing one word in your vocabulary, which word would it be?

174

If you could ask one yes or no question about your own death and have the answer now, what would you ask?

If you could have done one good deed that you had the opportunity to do but didn't, what would it be?

If you had to name the smartest person you have ever met, who would it be?

If you could make one thing come true for one friend, what would it be, and for whom?

If you had to identify the time or moment in your life when you felt the most free, when was it?

If you had to name the one personality trait that you have tried the hardest to change in yourself, what would you say?

If you had to name the most gentle person you know, who would it be?

If you could go back for one minute to the Garden of Eden and give Adam advice, what would you say?

176

If you could control the lens of a satellite for one hour, so that you could watch any spot on earth, where would you point it?

If you had to name the saddest thing you've ever witnessed, what would it be?

If you could have said one thing to Harry Truman the day before he decided to drop the atomic bomb, what would you have said?

If you lost feeling everywhere but in one small spot, where would you want the spot to be?

If you had to name the thing that most limits your freedom, what would it be?

If you could free yourself from one burden in your life, what would it be?

If you had to name the single best deed a stranger has done for you in your lifetime, what would it be?

If you could get God to do one thing to prove His existence, what would you ask Him to do to convince you?

178

If you could give an Academy Award to the most underappreciated actor in the history of Hollywood, who would you award it to?

--- ⚎◆⚎ ---

If you could have changed one thing about your mother's life, what would it be?

--- ⚎◆⚎ ---

If you had to name the most difficult good-bye you've ever said, what would it be?

If you could have one free service in your home every day, what would you take?

If you had to describe the silliest thing people do in general, what would you say?

———— ❊ ————

If you could guarantee one thing about your next trip, what would it be?

———— ❊ ————

If you could completely remove someone's vocal cords for a year, whose would they be?

———— ❊ ————

If you had to name the most incredible thing a friend has ever done for you, what would it be?

180

If you were given academic tenure to teach any course you wished at any university in the world, where would you want it to be, and in what subject?

If you had to be buried inside any existing tomb or grave, and the tomb's name would be changed to yours, whose would you want to take over?

— ⚔ —

If you could go back and fight any military battle differently, what battle would you pick, and how would you fight it?

— ⚔ —

If you had to name the one time when you truly went "beyond the call of duty," when would it be?

If you had to name the physical characteristic of your mate that most resembles their parents, what would it be?

If you could have any number of siblings, how many would you have, and of what gender?

If you had to name the best and worst diets you've ever tried, which would win and which would lose?

If you had to name the most beautiful spot on earth that you've ever seen, what would you choose?

If you had to name the single most important thing in your life, what would it be?

⸻ ✦ ⸻

If you had to say what one thing in your life best represents your freedom, what would it be?

⸻ ✦ ⸻

If you had to name the single most important duty of a parent, what would you say it is?

⸻ ✦ ⸻

If you had to identify what made the best teacher you ever had the best, what would you say it was?

183

If you could gain or lose weight in any one part of your body, where would it be?

—————⚜—————

If you could advise one couple you know to separate, who would it be?

If you could have prevented one thing from happening between a friend and yourself, what would it have been?

—————⚜—————

If the pope promised he would do one thing you asked of him, what would you ask?

If you had to name the grossest thing you have ever put in your mouth, what would it be?

If God were to whisper one thing in your ear, what would you like Him to say?

If you could do one thing that you've never done with a spray can of Reddi Whip, besides eat it, what would you do and to whom?

If you were to be asked the most difficult thing you can imagine by your best friend, what would it be?

If you could have asked Jesus Christ one thing just before the crucifixion, what would it have been?

If you could repair a relationship with one former friend, who would it be with?

If you had to predict which famous couple were going to separate next, who would you pick?

If you had to pick the worst driver you know, who would win?

If you asked the most difficult thing you can imagine of your lover, what would it be?

If you had to name the craziest thing you ever did in your youth, what would it be?

If you had to choose the most extreme example of sexual harassment you have suffered, what would it be?

If you could trade in-laws with anyone you know, whose would you take?

If you were to pick an object to be worshipped by a new religion, what would it be?

If you could retract one thing you've ever said, what would you take back?

———— ✦ ————

If you could tell any current world leader one thing as president of the United States, what would it be, and to whom would you say it?

———— ✦ ————

If you could ask the greatest sacrifice imaginable of a friend, what would it be?

If you were to identify the most important quality in a friend, what would you say it is?

‑‑ ⚜ ‑‑

If you had to pick the biggest Freudian slip you've ever made, what would it be?

‑‑ ⚜ ‑‑

If you had to repeat the worst thing you've ever said to your mother, what was it?

‑‑ ⚜ ‑‑

If you could have had more time together with someone you know, who would you want it to be with?

189

If you could have the chance to see what has become of one childhood friend, who would you choose to find out about?

If you had to name the single physical characteristic about yourself that most resembles your mother or father, what would it be?

If you had to nominate the best-dressed person you know, who would win?

If you had to name the one thing you envy most about your mate, what would it be?

190

If you had to name the most violent scene in a movie you have ever seen, what would it be?

If you could have had one thing that one of your friends has, what would you pick, and from whom?

If you could personally see one natural phenomenon that you have never seen, what would it be?

If you had to name the one person your mate knows who makes you jealous, who would it be?

191

If very good friends were visiting your town, where would you take them to eat if money were no object?

If you had to name the one thing that most easily makes your mate feel guilty, what would it be?

If you could take revenge on another driver, who would it be, and for what incident?

If you had to select one movie sequel that was superior to the original, what would it be?

If you could select a role model for each of your kids, who would you pick?

If you could completely redecorate any room in your house at someone else's expense, what room would you choose?

If you could decide how many times a year you saw your own parents, how often would it be?

If you could determine how often you see your in-laws, how often would it be?

193

If health were not an issue, how many times a month would you exercise?

If you had to describe the worst experience you've had in an automobile, what would it be?

—•— ⊨◊⊨ —•—

If you had to name the most overrated actor in Hollywood, who would it be?

—•— ⊨◊⊨ —•—

If you could open and run any kind of restaurant anywhere, what kind of food would you serve, and where?

194

If you had to name the three most important family values in order of importance, what would they be?

If you could have decided the outcome of the O. J. Simpson trial, what would your verdict be?

If you could have any single Hollywood celebrity be your slave for a weekend, who would you pick?

If you could have any single tabloid story actually come true, which one would it be?

If you could give a single piece of advice to the fashion industry right now, what would you say?

If you were on the committee to assign ratings to films, how would you define the categories?

＋・ ≡◆≡ ・＋

If you could have any single option added to your automobile, what would it be?

＋・ ≡◆≡ ・＋

If you could have one new store added to your local mall, what would it be?

196

If you could have prevented the bombing of any single city during a war in this century, which would it be?

If you could have participated in any march on Washington, which would you have been part of?

If you had known one thing that you didn't when you had your first sexual experience, what would it be?

If you had to name the one thing you did as a child to most torment your sibling(s), what was it that you did?

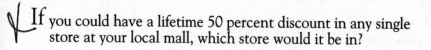

If you could have a lifetime 50 percent discount in any single store at your local mall, which store would it be in?

＋＋ ═◆═ ＋＋

If you were to have a weekend of sex with a person you would normally consider to be "beneath" you, who would you pick?

＋＋ ═◆═ ＋＋

If you were to pick the one child you know who you would predict to be the most successful in life, who would it be?

＋＋ ═◆═ ＋＋

If you could have been present at any one ticker-tape parade, which would you choose?

198

If you could have a copy of *The New York Times* from any single day in history, which would it be?

If you were Madonna, what would you do for your next publicity stunt?

If you could be given the complete film library of the work of a single actor, who would you pick?

If you could retract one expression of gratitude that you made erroneously, what would you take back?

199

If you could tell your mother or father one thing that you haven't, what would it be?

If you were invited to the White House for dinner tonight, what would you wear from your current wardrobe?

━━━ ≍◆≍ ━━━

If you had to name one person who should not have divorced their spouse, who would you pick?

━━━ ≍◆≍ ━━━

If you were to become a prostitute, how much money do you think you could charge per hour?

200

If you had to choose the hour of day when time goes slowest, what would you say?

＊—＋ ⊞◆⊞ ＋—＊

If you could have your spouse say one thing about you to friends, what would you want him or her to say?

＊—＋ ⊞◆⊞ ＋—＊

If you had to guess the one thing your mate says about you to friends, what would you say it is?

＊—＋ ⊞◆⊞ ＋—＊

If you had to identify the most extreme example of ingratitude you can think of from your own experiences, what would it be?

If you could freeze your mate's looks at one age, but you would grow older, what age would you pick?

+--- ≖◈≕ ---+

If you had to name the worst thing you've ever done to someone emotionally, what would it be?

+--- ≖◈≕ ---+

If you spoke English with a certain type of American accent other than your own, what would you want it to be?

+--- ≖◈≕ ---+

If you spoke English with a foreign accent, which would you want it to be?

202

If you had to name a song whose lyrics best captured an experience you had, which would it be?

<hr/>

If, from all the people you know, you were to pick a person whose name truly suits them, who would you choose?

If you could take back one gift you have given, but now wish you hadn't, what would it be?

<hr/>

If you could guarantee the happiness of any single person in the world because they most deserve it, who would it be?

203

If you had to choose the most beautiful name of an existing country, what would you choose?

If you could make someone you know less ignorant about one thing, who would you pick, and what would it be?

If every night you could have one singer appear to serenade you, who would you choose?

If you could learn the total number of hours you have spent in your life doing one thing, what would it be?

If you had to name the person you know with the best attitude regarding money, who would it be?

If you could have only one magazine subscription for life, which would you pick?

If you had to name the biggest hypocrite you have ever met, who would win?

If you could repeat one experience you had with your mate, what would it be?

205

If you could get a massage every day from one person, from whom would you want it to be?

If you could dedicate a song on the radio right now to your lover or spouse, which song would you pick?

If you had to nominate the worst-dressed person you know, who would it be?

If you had to choose the most necessary thing you do each day, what would you say it was?

If you could pair up any two single people you know, who would you pick?

If you were to decide on a new punishment for convicted murderers, aside from life imprisonment or the death penalty, what would it be?

If you could have your mate surprise you by doing one thing (other than give you a gift), what would you want them to do?

If you could fall asleep each night with your head resting upon anything other than your pillow, what would it be?

207

If you could choose someone you know to be a guest on a television show, who would it be, and on which show?

If you were to guess which of all the people you know platonically is the best in bed, who would you pick?

If you had to rely on one person you know in any difficult situation, who would you pick?

If you had to work in any store at your local mall, which would it be?

208

If you could have one extra hour each day to do only one thing, what would you do in that hour?

If you had a bust of yourself sculpted, where would you place it?

＋·　＝◆＝　·＋

If you had been Marcia Clark, what one thing would you have done differently in the O. J. Simpson trial?

＋·　＝◆＝　·＋

If your birthday could be in a different month of the year, when would you have it?

If you were to describe an act of true loyalty that you have witnessed, what would it be, and who performed it?

If you could arrange for one thing to happen to your spouse, without them knowing you arranged it, what would you plan?

If you could gain proof of someone's guilt about something, what would it be?

If you could destroy one thing physically, what would it be, and how would you do it?

If the laziest person you know had to do one thing each day for the rest of their life, who would it be, and what would they have to do?

◆—◆ ≡◆≡ ◆—◆

If you could teach one person you know a lesson about money, who would it be, and what would they learn?

If you could be more focused in one area of your life, what would it be?

◆—◆ ≡◆≡ ◆—◆

If you were to pick the most amoral person you know and teach them a single lesson, who and what would it be?

If you could rename every person in your family, what would they each be called?

⟶ ⫶✦⫶ ⟵

If you could have the lips of any living person, whose would you want?

⟶ ⫶✦⫶ ⟵

If you could avoid any one physical ailment in your old age, what would it be?

⟶ ⫶✦⫶ ⟵

If you could throw a great Halloween party anywhere, where would you have it?

212

If you had to name the best example of fate that you know, what would you say?

----- ≈◆≈ -----

If you could touch only one part of your own body for the rest of your life, where would you choose to touch?

If you had to name the book from your childhood that had the biggest influence on you, what book would it be?

----- ≈◆≈ -----

If you could punish the most difficult person you work with on a daily basis, what would you do, and to whom?

If you could have your license plate say anything at all, what would it be?

━━ ⚏✦⚏ ━━

If you had to pick the most beautiful word in your own language, what would you choose?

━━ ⚏✦⚏ ━━

If you had to describe yourself as a child in one word, what would it be?

━━ ⚏✦⚏ ━━

If you had to name a single song or album that you most associate with a particular period of your life, what song would you choose, and from what year?

214

If you had to describe the moment in your life when you had to have the most courage, what would you say?

If you could avoid ever having to see a certain relative again, who would it be?

✦

If you were to describe true generosity by using an example you witnessed, what would you use?

✦

If you had to recount your worst case of putting your foot in your mouth, when was it?

If you could go back and express gratitude about one thing in your life, for what would it be, and to whom?

If you were to give an award to someone for being the most moral person, who would win, and what would the award be?

If you were to name the person or people you have the most compassion for, who would it be?

If you could ask your best friend one question you have never had the nerve to ask, what would it be?

216

If you could have kept a detailed diary of one period of your life, so that you could now reread it, what period would it be from?

━━ ✦ ━━

If you had to name the one situation that would overwhelm your courage, what would it be?

━━ ✦ ━━

If you were to describe your first kiss, what would you say?

━━ ✦ ━━

If you devoted the next year to making as much money as possible above all else, how would you do it?

If you had to name the most difficult thing about being a teenager today, what would you say?

If you could change one thing about your love life, what would it be?

If you had to name the most embarrassing moment of your life, when was it?

If you could be given a personal tour of any Hollywood celebrity's house, whose would you want to see?

If you had to name the one thing you worried about most in high school, what was it, and did it merit all the fuss?

If you could make one change to your favorite mall, what would it be?

If you could modify your computer in any single way, how would you make it be different?

If you could find the personal diary of one person from history, with all the juicy details, whose would you want to find?

219

If you could define the legal limitations for pornography, what would you propose?

If you were to name the one possession that means the most to you, what would it be?

If you had to name a person who was the most important role model in your life, who would it be?

If the United States had to sacrifice one state, which one would you give away?

220

If you could communicate with any type of animal, which would you pick?

If you could have the sense of humor of anyone you know, whose would it be?

＋—— ▨◆▨ ——＋

If you had to name a time when you helped a stranger the most, when was it?

＋—— ▨◆▨ ——＋

If you had to recall the nicest compliment ever given to you, what would it be?

221

If you had to name the most difficult period of your life, when would it be?

If you could have a stranger come up to you and whisper anything into your ear, what would you want them to say?

If you could give one piece of advice to the Republican party, what would it be?

If you could implement a strategy to fight the war on drugs, what would it entail?

222

If you were to decide what legal rights gays and lesbians should have with regard to marriage and children, what would they be?

If you had to describe your most recurring dream, what would it be?

If you had to pick one of your personality traits as being the best, which would it be?

If you could havet one more pet, what kind would you get, and what would you name it?

If you had the gift of magic for one day, what would you do?

If you had to name the one thing that has changed the most about growing up since your childhood, what would it be?

If you could pump enormous amounts of money into one area of scientific research, what would it be for?

If you could force someone very rich to give away all their money for a single cause, who would you pick, and what cause would it go to?

If a one-year period of your diary were to be published, what year would you want it to be?

If you could have one person you have lost touch with call you up tonight and invite you to dinner, who would you want it to be?

If you had to name the one area of your life that you are the least self-disciplined in, what would it be?

If you could decide exactly how, when, and where your children would learn sex education, what would you consider to be ideal?

225

If you had to describe the perfect retirement home, what would it be like?

If you had to name the subject you took in school that turned out to be least useful or worthwhile, what would it be?

━━ ▆◆▆ ━━

If you could give one piece of advice to the Democratic party, what would it be?

━━ ▆◆▆ ━━

If you were asked to define what a feminist is in one sentence, what would your response be?

226

If you could be sainted for doing one thing in life, what would it be for?

If you could change one thing about your marriage, what would you alter?

If you could establish criteria for the right to be a parent, what would they be?

If you could enact one law that applied only to your own family, what would it be?

227

If you could revise the current parole laws, what would you want to do?

If you could have named the first woman something other than Eve, what name would you pick?

If you could have named the first man something other than Adam, what would you pick?

If you could own a single prop from any film ever made, what would you choose?

If you could have done one thing with one of your teachers, what would it be, and with whom?

If you could retrieve one toy or stuffed animal from your childhood, which one would you recover?

If you could wake up tomorrow in your own bed next to anyone or anything, who or what would it be?

If you could do one thing to revise the welfare system, what would you do?

229

If you had to name a person you know who would be the easiest to seduce, who would it be?

If you were to have the voice of one media personality, whose would it be?

If you could have God perform one miracle today, what would you wish it to be?

If you could regulate (or deregulate) smoking, what rules would you make (or repeal)?

If you could receive more affection from someone you know from now on, who would you want it to be from?

If you could look through anyone's personnel file at work, whose would you pick?

If you had to recall the one time in your childhood or adolescence when you made your parents the most angry, when was it?

If you could reform the health care system right now, how would you do it?

231

If you had to name the one thing you have done that most pleased your parents, what would you say?

—————◄◆►—————

If you had to name the person who most objected to your choice of mate, who would it be?

—————◄◆►—————

If you could do one thing right now that isn't being done to help solve the problem of AIDS, what would it be?

If you could own one article of clothing from any film ever made, what would you take?

If you were to sleep with any famous couple, who would you choose?

━━━ ━◆━ ━━━

If you had to name the issue that will be the most important in the next election, what would you say?

━━━ ━◆━ ━━━

If you could have studied one subject in school that you didn't, or that wasn't offered, what would it be?

━━━ ━◆━ ━━━

If you had to have one job that you have had previously, which one would you want again?

If you were to name the greatest sexual advantage that women have over men, what would it be?

If your community decided to build low-cost housing, where would you propose it be located?

＋—＊—＋

If you could have the autograph of any athlete you do not have, whose would it be, and what would you like them to sign?

＋—＊—＋

If you could set the guidelines for gun control, what would they be?

If you were given the power to settle the issue of gays in the military, what policy would you set?

If you had to name the best sexual advantage that men have over women, what would it be?

If you could have the original baseball card of any three players in history, who would they be?

If you could relive any single family outing in your life, what would it be?

235

If you had to pick one foreign language that students would be required to learn in school, what would it be?

If you could set the national speed limit for all highways, what would it be?

If you could sit and have a beer with three sports figures from any time, who would you pick?

If you could be emotionally closer to one member of your family, who would it be?

236

If you had to pick the member of your family who is least like the others, who would it be?

If you had to pick the worst teacher from your childhood, who would win the prize?

If you were to describe your favorite sexual fantasy, what would it be?

If you were in charge of the military budget, what is the first thing you would do?

237

If you had to choose the person from your family you most admire, who would it be?

—✦—

If you were six inches tall for a day, what would you do?

—✦—

If you could have anyone in the world stop by for a visit, who would you want it to be?

If the world were to turn to one single source of energy tomorrow, what would you want it to be?

If you had to pick the teacher you've had who would be the most disappointed with how your life turned out, who would it be?

— ⚔ —

If you had to name the world's most pressing environmental concern, what would it be?

— ⚔ —

If you had to pick the most embarrassing thing your parents did to you as a child, what was it?

— ⚔ —

If you could have one television sitcom set as your real home, which show would it be from?

239

If you were to have someone's autograph tattooed somewhere on your body, whose would it be, and where would you put it?

If you could rename any sports team, which would you pick, and what would you rename it?

If you could add one required course to the present school system, what would it be?

If you could revise the income tax system, what would you propose?

If you could have the personality of any TV character, whose would you adopt?

If you could pass one law to help the environment, what would it be?

If you could retake one course you took in high school or college, which would it be?

If you could make one change to your garden, what would it be?

241

If you were to set your country's immigration policy, what would it be?

If you were to describe the worst poverty you have ever seen, what would you say?

If you could grow the world's most perfect specimen of plant or flower, what would it be?

If you could impose a heavy luxury tax on any single item, what would it be?

If you could go back to high school to relive one event exactly as it happened, what would you pick?

If you could go back to high school to relive one event as you wish it had been, what would it be?

If you were to name the most ridiculous lawsuit you have ever heard about, what would it be?

If you were to select the person you know who would be the most difficult to seduce, who would you name?

243

If you could spend next New Year's Eve doing anything, what would you do, and with whom?

–•–••–

If you could have been present during the inauguration of any past president, whose would it be?

–•–••–

If you could un-tax anything now currently taxed, what would you pick?

–•–••–

If you could have season tickets for any team, sitting in any place in the stadium, which team would it be and where would you sit?

If you were to spend a week anywhere alone without contact with civilization, where would you go?

If you could ski in any place in the world, where would you go?

If you had to choose a television personality to be president of the United States, who would you pick?

If you could be caressed by the hands of any person you have known platonically, whose would they be?

If you had to name the person you know with the sexiest phone voice, who would win?

If you could relocate your entire workplace to a new location, where would you want it to be?

If you were to be the first lady (or first man), what would you want your role to be?

If you had to be stuck for hours in any airport, which would you want it to be in?

If you could spend an entire day in any zoo by yourself, which zoo would you pick to be in, and what would you do?

If you could have an entire city depopulated to explore with a friend for one week, what city would it be, and what would you do?

If you had to recall your worst travel experience, what would it be?

If you had to give up one of your vices for Lent next year, which would you sacrifice?

If you could make one person jealous, who would it be, and how would you do it?

If you had to guess that two people at work were having an affair, who would you pair?

If you did not work, how much TV would you watch every day?

If you had to pick the TV personality you were most in love with as a kid, who would it be?

If you were to make any hotel room your home for a year, where would it be?

────── ✦ ──────

If you could live in a past era just so you could wear the clothes in fashion at the time, when would it be?

────── ✦ ──────

If you could redesign the uniforms of any sports team, which team would it be, and what changes would you make?

────── ✦ ──────

If you could kiss anyone in the world on one spot other than the lips, who would you choose, and where would you kiss them?

If you had to name the best speech given at the Academy Awards, whose was it?

If God were to appear before you in any form, what form would you want Him to take?

——⋈◆⋈——

If you were to give anyone a raise at work (other than yourself), who would you give it to?

——⋈◆⋈——

If you had to name the hardest position to play in sports, what would you say it is?

If you could frame the jockstrap of any sports figure and hang it in your den, whose would you choose?

If you had to describe the thing done by someone at work that drives you the craziest, what would you say?

If you had to name the next person who should be fired at your place of employment, who would you choose?

If you were to name one person you know who is a true gentleman, who would it be?

251

If you were to define the word *courage* by giving an example, how would you do it?

***

If you had to pick the one institution you have the most faith in, what would you say?

***

If you were to be the opposite sex for a single day, what would you do?

***

If you could play a prank on anyone at work with impunity, what would you do, and to whom?

252

If you could go back to one place you have been in your life, where would you go?

If you had to be addicted to one thing, what would it be?

—◆—

If you were to have the hands of someone you know, whose would you want?

—◆—

If you could remove the ability to hate from one person in the world today, who would it be?

If you could be any sign of the zodiac other than your own, what would you want to be?

If you could run any existing charity, which would it be?

If you could insist that one person you work with deliver coffee to you every day, who would you chose?

If you could have taken part in any single historical ceremony, what would it have been?

254

If you were to name the one choice in life that you would never want to make again, what would it be?

If you had to disguise yourself physically, how would you do it?

If you could have one science fiction story come true, which would it be?

If you had to have the hair of a current politician, whose would you pick?

If you could remove one marking from your skin, which one would it be?

If you had to choose, from among your current friends, one person to be your partner in a new business venture, who would you choose?

If you were to name the most obnoxious tourists you've encountered, who would they be?

If you had to eliminate forever one form of weather, what would it be?

256

If you could go back to an incident in your past, in order to act more honorably than you did, what situation would it be?

If you could gain back all the hours you've spent in your life doing a certain thing, what would it be?

<hr>

If you could have one piece of jewelry belonging to someone you know personally, what would you pick?

<hr>

If you could ensure one thing about Heaven besides its existence, what would it be?

257

If you were to get a divorce, what is the one thing you would fight for above all else (besides your children)?

—+— ≡◆≡ —+—

If you could have had any job in history, what would it have been?

—+— ≡◆≡ —+—

If you could ensure that one existing law would never be broken by anyone, which would it be?

—+— ≡◆≡ —+—

If you could go back in time to undo one injury you inflicted on someone else, what would it be?

258

If you had to name the one person you have been most jealous of, who would win?

If you had to name the one thing about your life right now that you would not change, what would it be?

If you could receive a kiss from anyone in the world on one part of your body other than your lips, who would you want to kiss you, and where?

If you could forget one thing, what would it be?

259

If³...

(Questions for the Game of Love)

The authors would like to dedicate this book
to all those who have given them love,
and who have received theirs.

Love. Romance. Sex.

From the imaginative lover to the imaginary one, our *imaginations* play a central role in our love lives. Pity the person who believes there exists no connection between the heart and the imagination, or pity their lover, anyway. From the first time we begin to discover there's a thing called love—tumultuous, chaotic, confusing, frightfully powerful, and stunningly joyous—we begin to imagine what might be if . . .

And as long as we are able to love (in other words, as long as we are alive), our imaginations help us through it, fill in the gaps, make us hopeful, steel our nerves, augment our romantic ideas, protect our humility, guide our actions, and help keep things interesting. Would we dare enter into love otherwise?

Yet as wonderful and wrenching as romantic love can be, it remains startlingly incomprehensible, and the mysteries of our own hearts tantalize us. Can we know more? Are we meant to? Ask yourself some of these questions, and ask those you love, or would like to. Where will they take you? What will they reveal? Do you have the courage to answer? Be prepared for anything.

And always, always, treasure the game of love.

We would like to add that some of the following questions are rather direct, and personal, and not everyone will choose to ponder them, but in no case do we intend offense.

If you were to complete the phrase "A life without love . . . ," how would you finish it?

•—◆—•

If you had to have sex simultaneously with two people you know, who would you want them to be?

If you could have anyone in the world say one romantic thing to you, what would it be, and who would utter it?

•—◆—•

If you could make love one more time with someone from your past, who would you choose?

If you had to watch your lover or spouse have sex with someone else, but could determine who it would be, who would you choose?

·—· ▤◆▤ ·—·

If you could personally undress anyone you know that you have never seen naked, who would you disrobe?

·—· ▤◆▤ ·—·

If you could kiss—but only kiss—one person you know anytime you wanted, who would it be?

·—· ▤◆▤ ·—·

If you had to name the most sensual part of your own body, what would you pick?

266

If you wanted to nonverbally signal to your lover in public that you wanted to make love, how would you do it?

If you could have a sensuous massage every day from someone famous, who would you choose?

If you could grab the buttocks of someone famous, whose would you grab?

If you wanted to turn your lover on as quickly as possible, what means would you use?

If you had to repeat the sexiest words anyone has ever said to you, what would they be?

If you were to identify the biggest turn-off in sex, what would you say it was?

If you went back in time to have sex with someone from your high school that you didn't have sex with then, who would you pick?

If from now on you could only have sex at a certain time of the day, when would it be?

268

If you were to have oral sex with someone famous right now, who would it be?

━◆═◆━

If you could receive a sexual proposition from any one person, who would it be, and how would you want them to do it?

━◆═◆━

If you were to name the most romantic thing you've ever done for someone else, what would it be?

If you were to define "kinky," how would you do it?

If you had to select the sexiest word in the English language, what would you say it is?

--- ✦ ---

If you had to involve (directly) one type of food in your next sexual act, what would it be?

If you had to pick the person with the hottest body you know but have never slept with, who would you say has it?

--- ✦ ---

If you could change one thing about the way your lover makes love, what would it be?

If you could try one thing in bed that you've never done, what would it be?

⊷ ≡◆≡ ⊶

If you had to choose the person with the most remarkable sexual reputation of anyone you've known, who would win?

⊷ ≡◆≡ ⊶

If you were to pick the worst misogynist you know, who would you say it is?

⊷ ≡◆≡ ⊶

If you had to name the most extreme man-hater you know, who would it be?

If you had to name the most erotic book you have ever read, what would you pick?

If you had to describe the sexiest dream you've ever had, which one would qualify?

—✦—

If you could have lost your virginity to someone you have met since, who would it be?

—✦—

If you were to name the sexiest part of your mate's body, what would it be?

272

If you had to name the noisiest person you have ever had sex with, who would it be?

—•— ⚎◆⚎ —•—

If you were to name the one part of your body you most like to touch, what would it be?

—•— ⚎◆⚎ —•—

If you were to describe the kinkiest thing you would do under the right circumstances, what would it be?

—•— ⚎◆⚎ —•—

If you were to name the person you've made love with who was the biggest surprise (for better or for worse) in bed, who would you say it was?

273

If you had to name the biggest turn-on you have experienced in the history of your sex life, what would it be?

If you were to name the most romantic moment in your life so far, what would you say?

If you were to recall the most humorous thing that has happened to you in bed, what would it be?

If you could have changed one thing about the first time you had sex, what would you alter?

If you were to name a person whose attraction toward you is incomprehensible, who would it be?

If you were to think of a couple you know about whom you would say, "What on earth is he doing with her [or she with him]?," who would it be?

If you were to think of a famous couple about whom you would say, "What on earth are they doing together?," who would it be?

If there was one moment in the history of your love life when you were truly scared of the situation you were in, when would it be?

If you had to pick your best masturbation fantasy, what would it involve?

―――――•≡◆≡•―――――

If you had to choose the best music to make love to, what would you pick?

If, for the rest of your life, you could achieve an instant orgasm by being touched on one particular spot on your body, where would you want it to be?

―――――•≡◆≡•―――――

If you could be amazing at only one specific thing in bed, what would you want it to be?

276

If you had to hear one barnyard sound every time you had an orgasm, what would it be?

If you could change one thing about your lover's private parts, what would you change?

If you had to smell one food every time you had sex, for the rest of your life, what would it be?

If you could have any opera singer personally sing you a romantic aria, who would it be, and what would they sing?

277

If you could have changed one thing about your most recent sexual experience, what would it be?

If you had to name your favorite place to masturbate, where would it be?

If you were to repeat the most romantic thing anyone has written to you in a letter, what would it be, and by whom?

If you had to pick the most romantic moment in any film from history, what would you say?

If you had to name the "dirtiest" thing you have ever done, what would qualify?

If you could have your lover experience one thing you do that they now can't, what would it be?

If you could have videotaped any sexual experience you've ever had, which would you choose to record?

If you were to name the person who lost their virginity at the youngest age you know, who would it be?

279

If you were to repeat the funniest nicknames you have ever heard for each of the private parts, what would they be?

If you were to talk about the greatest lips you have ever kissed, how would you describe them?

If you were to name the best place that you ever made love, where would you say it was?

If you could have changed one thing about your own wedding ceremony, what would be revised?

280

If you were to decorate one room (secretly if you prefer) in your house, solely devoted to your erotic life, what would you put in it?

If you were to name the sexiest hotel room you have ever stayed in, which would you pick?

If you were to pick the most romantic city or foreign country you know, which would win?

If you were going to elope tonight, where would you go?

If you had to recall the riskiest place you've ever had sex, where would it be?

If you were to select the moment in your life when you looked the sexiest, when would it be?

If you were to pick a moment when your mate looked the sexiest they ever have, when would it be?

If you were to name the woman you know who has most enjoyed her pregnancy, who would it be?

If you were to pick the best and worst wedding presents you got, what would they be, and from whom?

If you had to describe the most erotic thing men can wear, what would you say?

If you could "unknow" any sexual fact, what would you choose?

If you had to have one television show on while you were making love, which one would you want?

If you had to pick the best advice that someone gave you at, or about, your own wedding, what was it, and who said it?

If you had to confess the dirtiest thing you've ever done in the dark of a movie theater, what would you say?

If you could have sex in any single make of automobile, which would you choose?

If you had to name the dumbest place you've ever had sex, where would it be?

284

If you had to have one part of your anatomy dyed permanently blue, what part would you pick?

If you were to choose the person you find quite sexy despite being otherwise unattractive, who would you pick?

If you had to name the one person who most truly tested your sexual self-restraint, who would it be?

If you could do one physical thing to your lover while they slept, without them knowing about it at the time, what would you do?

If you had to have given any one person a sexual affliction, who would you have given it to, and what would it be?

--- ❖ ---

If you could have a photo of any one moment from your wedding that was not recorded, what would it be of?

--- ❖ ---

If you could invite a celebrity to join you in a threesome, who would you want?

--- ❖ ---

If you could give back one thing a lover gave you, what would it be?

286

If you could lose your virginity over again to someone famous, who would you want it to be?

━◆━

If you had to pick the two people you would least like to watch having sex together who currently do, who would they be?

If you were to make love in a public place, where would it be?

━◆━

If you were to have any author write a novel about your love life, who would you have do it?

If you could plan your ideal honeymoon, what would it entail?

If you could have any single view from your bed, what would it be?

If you could pick the last person you will ever make love to, who would you select?

If you could invent a new method of birth control, what would it be like?

If you could go back and give one thing to a past lover, who would you choose, and what would you give?

If you could take back one thing you ever said in a romantic situation, what would it be?

If you could have made one person fall in love with you, who would you pick?

If you could have someone you know fall in love with someone else, who would they be?

If you could change the sexual practices of anyone you know, who would it be, and how would you change them?

If you could change one tradition regarding marriage, what would it be?

If you had to name the one thing you wear that makes you look sexy, what would you say it is?

If you were to hire an escort tonight, what type of person would you request, and what services would you ask for?

If you had to be the mattress of one famous person, whose would you want to be?

If you were to carry with you at all times a plaster cast of one part of your lover's face or body, what part would it be?

If you could temporarily freeze the world and everyone in it (except yourself), what sexual things would you do, and to whom?

If you were planning your wedding now and could hold it anywhere you wanted, where would you have it?

If you had to describe the kinkiest thing you've ever done, what would you say?

If you could go back and change one thing about your wedding night after the guests were all gone, what would you alter?

＊＊＊

If your best friends were to hire an escort for you without warning you beforehand, what qualities do you think they would request?

＊＊＊

If you were to plan your version of the perfect pre-wedding party (stag/bachelorette) for your next wedding, what would be included?

292

If you had to have one of your friends always give you the intimate details of their love life, who would you wish it to be?

If you could go back and say one thing to someone you were infatuated with in school, what would you say, and to whom?

If you were to name the person you most regret ever having kissed, who would get the prize?

If you could hear the unedited fantasies of anyone you know, whose would you want to listen to?

If you could hear the romantic fantasies of anyone famous, who would you select?

--- ◆ ---

If you could reach any part of your own body to kiss that you can't now, what would it be?

--- ◆ ---

If you could change the sexual attitudes of anyone you know, who would it be?

--- ◆ ---

If you were to photograph yourself in a sexy pose, what pose would you strike?

294

If you had to give the age of the youngest person you've ever slept with, what would it be?

—◦—◆—◦—

If you had to give the age of the oldest person you've ever slept with, what would it be?

—◦—◆—◦—

If you had to pick the age of the youngest and oldest people you *would* ever sleep with, how old would they be?

If you were to name the part of other people's bodies you most like to touch, what would it be?

If you had to use one household substance as a sexual lubricant (that you have never before used), what would you try?

If you could have known one thing about your spouse on your wedding day that you have learned since, what would it be?

If you had to pick one friend to plan your stag or bachelorette party, who would you want to do it?

If you were to name the company that has the most sensual advertisements, who would win?

296

If you were to confess the most embarrassing moment in your sexual history, what would it be?

If you had to pick the closest you have ever come to being caught in the act, when would it be?

If you were to pick the greatest single day in your sexual history, what would it be?

If you were to name the most erotic person you see regularly that you know you will never sleep with, who would it be?

If you had to name the nationality who make the best lovers, in your own experience, what would you say?

If you could have your lover say one thing to you more often than they do (and mean it), what would you want to hear?

If you could have returned the love of someone you rejected in the past, who would it be?

If you had to put a new sexually explicit tattoo on your body, where would you have it located, and what would it be?

298

If every time you had sex a big bell would chime somewhere in the world, where would you want it to be?

If everyone in the world had to donate one dollar to charity every time they had sex, how long do you think it would take to wipe out poverty?

— ✠ —

If you could have said one thing during your wedding ceremony that you didn't, what would it be?

— ✠ —

If you were to recall the dumbest thing you said at your wedding, what would it be?

299

If there was one spot on your lover's body that had to be put permanently off-limits to your touch, where would you want it to be?

<hr />

If every man on Earth had to have genitals identical to those of someone you have known, whose would you pick?

<hr />

If you had to name one thing ever said to you by a lover that you wish hadn't been, what would it be?

<hr />

If you were to recall the strangest physical thing you've ever had happen during lovemaking, how would you describe it?

300

If, for the rest of your life, you had to always eat the same meal right before you had sex, what would you want it to include?

If you were to pick the sexiest advertisement of all time, which would you say it was?

If you could have freckles on one part of your body that you don't, where would they be?

If you could remove one birthmark or scar from your body, which would it be?

301

If you could have any poet from history write a love poem to you, who would you pick?

If you were to choose the best meal to be eaten right after making love, what would it be?

If you could have invited anyone you didn't to your own wedding, who would it be?

If you could have *not* invited anyone you had to (and did) to your own wedding, who would it be?

If you had to pick your best "making-up" after a lovers' quarrel, when would it be?

If you had to recall the person who was the most difficult to face the morning after, who would it be?

If you had to pick the person you've known or met who, with charisma alone, could have seduced you, who would it be?

If you had to choose your own sexiest characteristic, what would it be?

If your mate were to give you a new tattoo while you were sleeping, where would they most likely place it, and what would it be of?

If you had to pick the one person in your life you have felt the strongest platonic love for, aside from members of your family, who would you say it was?

If you could plan your own fiftieth wedding anniversary, what would it be like?

If you were to name the two people you know who come closest to being soul mates, who would they be?

304

If you were to win an award for the time you made the most noise during sex, what occasion would be cited, and who were you with at the time?

If you could have objected at any wedding and put a halt to it, whose would it have been?

＋—━◆━—＋

If you were to put one spot of your body off-limits to your lover's touch, where would it be?

＋—━◆━—＋

If your lover could do one thing to you while you slept, without waking you up, what do you think they'd do?

If you could convert one heterosexual to homosexuality, who would you choose, and would it be temporary or permanent?

If you could convert one homosexual to heterosexuality, who would it be, and would it be for a day or a lifetime?

If you were to ask someone you love for a single proof of their love for you, what would you demand?

If you were to pick the most beautiful wedding ceremony you've ever been to, whose would you say it was?

If the feelings you experience in your genitals during orgasm could be replicated in one other part of your body every time you did one nonsexual thing, where would you want to feel it, and during what activity?

***

If you had to remember every person you've ever had sex with, how accurate could you be?

If you were to give a prize for the silliest name for sexual intercourse, what would win?

***

If you could only make love in one position for the rest of your life, which position would you want it to be?

If you could have had anyone from history show up at your wedding, who would you have wanted it to be?

—————◼◆◼—————

If you had to name the most beautiful wedding dress you've ever seen, whose would it be?

—————◼◆◼—————

If you were to describe the most romantic letter or note you have ever written, what would you say?

—————◼◆◼—————

If you were to name one spot on your body where you always like to be touched, what would it be?

308

If you were to pick the sexiest season for clothes, what would it be?

If any person you chose in the world accepted your offer of payment to watch them having sex, who would it be, and what's the most you would pay them?

If your lover asked you to do one thing (of your choice) that you've never done before, in order to prove your love for them, what would you do?

If you were asked to add one phrase or statement to all marriage ceremonies, what would you add?

If you had to name the two people you know who should most be a couple but aren't, who would you pick?

⸺ ❖ ⸺

If you had to name the one spouse or mate of a friend you have most lusted after, who would it be?

⸺ ❖ ⸺

If you could try one sexual position you never have, which one would it be?

⸺ ❖ ⸺

If you could receive a love letter from anyone alive, who would it be from?

310

If you had to pick the worst quarrel you have ever had with a lover, what was it about, and who was it with?

If you were to devise a test to determine whether people were true soul mates, what would it entail?

If you could write (or rewrite) a prenuptial agreement for your own marriage, what would it say?

If you were asked to state at what age a person is ready to have sexual intercourse, how would you answer?

If you were now given ten dollars for every time you had masturbated in your life until the present, how radically would you be able to upgrade your standard of living?

—————◄◆►—————

If you could have attended any famous couple's wedding, whose would you choose?

—————◄◆►—————

If you were to demand one thing from your next divorce (other than money or children), what would you ask for?

—————◄◆►—————

If you were to guess what the most popular sex toy is, what would you say?

312

If you had to have the voice of someone you know coaching you in a whisper every time you had sex for the rest of your life, whose voice would you want it to be?

If you could see one romantic film again, which would it be?

—————————

If the genitals of the entire opposite sex were to have the aroma of one food item, what would you pick?

—————————

If you had to guess the average age that people today lose their virginity, what would you say?

If you could send a love letter to anyone alive and know that they would receive and read it, who would it be addressed to?

If you had to name the most romantic gift you have ever given, what would it be?

If you had to describe the best romantic gift you have ever received, what would it be, and from whom?

If you could write something to one of your lovers that would be opened and read by them only after you die, who would it be to, and what would it say?

If you could teach your children one moral lesson about love, what would it be?

If you were to name the one person you know who is lacking sound judgment about their own relationship, who would it be?

If you could eliminate one marital problem for everyone on Earth, what would you choose?

If you were to name the greatest regret of your romantic life, what would it be?

315

If you were to name the person you have known with the shallowest definition of love, who would you pick, and how would they define it?

If you were to name the person you know who has been married the most often, who would it be?

If you could ensure one thing about your children's love life, what would it be?

If you had to name the best wedding gift you've ever heard of (besides money), what would it be?

316

If you could have one domestic chore also be an erotic act, which would you choose?

If you had to name the person you had your biggest childhood or adolescent crush on, who would it be?

If you had to name the person you know that you'd least like to sleep with right now, who would it be?

If you had to say how many times you've had sex, what would be your best guess?

If you were to pick the person who had the easiest pregnancy, who would it be?

If you were to pick the person who had the most difficult pregnancy, who would it be?

If you were to name the TV show with the most sexual imagery ever, which would it be?

If you could find out something about your lover's sex life before you knew them, what would you ask about?

318

If you were to pick the sport that develops the sexiest body type, which would it be?

If you were to select the most sensual dancer you have had the pleasure of dancing with, who would you pick?

If you were to name a person who you think needs to "come out of the closet," who would it be?

If you were to make your most seductive face, what would you look like?

If you were to select the most romantic book ever written, which would it be?

If you were to name the sexiest actor and actress ever, who would you choose?

If you had to name the least sexy actor and actress ever, who would it be?

If you had to repeat the most ridiculous thing you have ever uttered during sex, what was it, and who were you with?

320

If you were to name a place you would like to make love in that you haven't, what would it be?

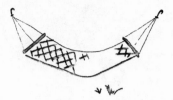

If you were to rate your love life as it is right now, on a scale from 1 to 10, what number would you choose?

If you were to select the most romantic restaurant you know, which would qualify?

If you were to describe the best thing any lover can do in the morning, what would it entail?

321

If you were to articulate the biggest difference between the way a woman loves a man and the way a man loves a woman, what would you say?

If you found your true love, how long would you *truly* wait for them to return your love?

If you were to name the one thing about your love life that you are most ashamed of, what would you say?

If you were to name a person in your life who you were attracted to but should not have been for some reason, who would it be, and why?

If you were to name the person you know with the most exaggerated opinion of their own attractiveness, who would you say it is?

If you were to remember one romantic experience that changed your life, what would you say?

If you were to choose the one thing that most convinced you that the person you are with is the right person to be with, what would you say?

If you were to name the one thing that in the past gave you the strength to leave a lover, what would you say?

323

If you were to name the one romantic lover in your life that you have shed the most tears over, who would it be?

If you were to name the two people you know who took the longest time to break up, who would they be?

If you could shave anyone's entire body, whose would you pick?

If you could have your body shaved by anyone, who would you want to do it?

If you were to choose the one material object that could best express or represent love, what would it be?

If you were to choose the most sensual room you have ever been in, what space would you pick?

If you were to choose the one type of women's makeup that is the best turn-on, what would you select?

If you were to choose the best wedding cake you have ever tasted, at whose wedding was it served?

If you were to name one person (more than any other) who you now cannot believe you were ever attracted to, who would it be?

If you were to name one person in your life who you will never have the right opportunity to say "I love you" to, who would it most likely be?

If you were to select the person you know who has broken the most hearts, who would you say it is?

If you were to name a person whose heart you truly broke, who would it be?

326

If you were to name the most bizarre fetish of anyone you know, what is it, and who has it?

If you were to name the most surprising place you have heard that someone you know has had sex, what would you say?

⸻✦⸻

If you were to define the perfect marriage in a few simple sentences, how would you do it?

⸻✦⸻

If you were to define the perfect divorce, what would you say?

If you had to name the man who has impregnated the most women, who would you guess it to be?

If you were to recall your longest climax ever, how long did it last, and how did it come about?

If you were to say what the best thing about starting a new relationship is, what would it be?

If you wanted to be aroused over the telephone by someone other than your current lover, who would be best at it?

If you were to plan a romantic evening that did not include sex, what would it be like?

⊷ ⬧ ⊶

If you were to continue the quotation "How do I love thee? Let me count the ways . . . ," what would "the ways" be for you in your current relationship?

⊷ ⬧ ⊶

If you could eliminate one emotion that has to do with romance, what would you get rid of?

⊷ ⬧ ⊶

If you were to name a person that you believe has never experienced true love, who would it be?

329

If you were to set regulations for pornography on the Internet, what would you propose?

If you could have anything occur on every wedding anniversary, what would you want to happen?

If you could pass one new national law related to sex, what would you ask for?

If you were to remember the quickest quickie you have ever had, just how quick was it?

330

If you were to choose the most difficult thing about ending a relationship, what would it be?

If you could give your kids one piece of advice about marriage that they would follow, what would you say?

If you could find out any single sexual statistic, what would you want to know?

If you could have found out something about sex sooner than you did, what would it be?

If you were to make one change to your home to improve your love life, what would you alter?

If you were to name an actor that others find sexy but you just don't, who would it be?

━━◆━━

If you could hire an escort for a friend, who would it be for, and what services would you order for them?

━━◆━━

If you had to name the person you know who is most afraid of romantic love, who would you say it is?

332

If you were to name the most insulting thing ever said to you by a lover, what would it be?

If you could give a prize for lovemaking to one person you have known, who would win it, and what would the prize be?

If you had to pick the most clever thing you've ever done in revenge, what would win?

If you had to accompany one couple you know on their honeymoon, who would you join?

If you were to prescribe the best cure for lovesickness, what would it be?

If you had to come up with just one word to describe each of your past lovers, what would it be?

If you had to choose a meal that best represented your love life, what would be on the menu, and where would you eat it?

If you were to recall one specific period of your life when you masturbated the most, when would it be?

If you had to pick the person it was the most difficult to break up with, who would it be?

If you were to name the two people who took the longest to finally commit to each other, who would they be?

If you had to say one thing you told somebody about your love life that you now wish you hadn't, what would it be?

If you were to name one person you had enormous luck in seducing, who would it be?

If you were to use a metaphor right now to sum up your love life, what would you say?

If you could buy any sex toy for yourself, what would it be, what would you name it, and how much would you pay for it?

If you could make love only one day of the year, which day would you choose?

If you could forget one year of your romantic life, which one would you erase from your memory?

336

If you were to invent a replacement for the tradition of the wedding ring, what would it be?

···◄◆►···

If you were to guess the thing that would most surprise you about your parents' sex lives, what would it be?

···◄◆►···

If you were to describe the single most kinky thing you think your mate would do, what would you say?

If you had to name the most humiliating moment you have had involving a lover, what would you say?

337

If you were to pick the lover you have had who had the most beautiful sexual organ, who would win?

If you were to guess which of your lovers had the highest sperm count, who would it be?

If all of your ex-lovers were to say the same romantic thing about you, what would you prefer it to be?

If you had to confess one thing about your love life to your mother, what would you say to her?

If you could meet with one lover from your past right now to see how they are, who would you want it to be?

—◆═◆═◆—

If you were to pick a food that is the most sensual while being eaten, what would it be, and who would you love to watch eating it?

If you could have known everything one former lover did while out of your sight, which person would you pick?

—◆═◆═◆—

If you had to see, for the rest of your life, an image of someone you've known, while you are having sex, whose face would it be?

339

If you were to name a person you would like to watch while they are masturbating, who would you pick?

⋯⋯ ⊞♦⊞ ⋯⋯

If you were to state the longest length of time that lust for one single person can sustain itself, how long would you say it is, and under what conditions?

⋯⋯ ⊞♦⊞ ⋯⋯

If you were to remember the shortest romance you have ever had, which would it be?

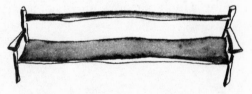

If you were to decide the best place to make love other than a bed, what would you say?

If you were to describe the saddest love story between two people that you know personally, what would you say?

If you were to name the most difficult "I love you" that you ever had to say, who did you say it to, and why was it so difficult?

If you were to name the situation where you had to fight the hardest to keep a person at bay, what would it be?

If you had to admit to one time when you were overcome with sheer animalistic lust for someone, what would you say?

341

If all of your children, gathered together, told you that they were gay, what would your reaction be?

If your daughter told you she was pregnant and didn't know who the father was, what advice would you give her?

If you had to name both the hardest and easiest people to give affection to that you know, who would they be?

If you had to name the type of weather you find the most romantic, what would you say?

342

If you had to name the cutest romantic habit your lover has, what would you say?

If you had to name the most lethargic person in bed you ever knew, who would it be?

If you had to name the one thing you most fear about relationships, what would it be?

If you had to pick one smell you most readily associate with sex, what would it be?

If you could leave just one photograph of you and your spouse (that you already have) for the rest of your family to have forevermore, which one would it be?

If you had to name the one incident that truly made you question your love for your mate, what would it be?

If you were to think of the biggest misconception about marriage, what would it be?

If you were forced to choose one thing more important in life than love, what would you pick?

344

If every time you masturbated in the next year you had to be observed by one person you know platonically, who would you pick?

If you had to imitate the strangest sound anyone ever made while making love, what sound would you make?

If one food for you could be an aphrodisiac, which food would you select?

If you were to identify a true symptom of lovesickness, what would you say it is?

If you had to name a person you know about whom you would say, "They are very sexy for their age," who would it be?

—✦—

If you had to name the person who makes really great sounds during lovemaking, who would it be?

—✦—

If you were to pick the relationship in which you faked more orgasms than any other, which would it be?

—✦—

If you had to name the person you've never had to fake an orgasm with, who would it be?

346

If you had to guess the person you work with who is most likely to wear sexy underwear, who would it be?

If you had to name the one part of the human body—besides the sexual organs—that you consistently find sexy, what part would it be?

--- ❖ ---

If you were to imagine one thing your lover could confess to you that would make you extremely upset, what would it be?

--- ❖ ---

If you had to guess which of your friends' children will grow up to be the sexiest looking, who would you choose?

If you had to guess which person, among all those you know, is the kinkiest in private, who would it be?

If you had to guess who, among the people you know, would be the most disappointing in bed, who would be the one?

If you had to pick, from all the cars you've owned, the best one to make out in, which would it be?

If you had to admit to the raunchiest thing you have ever done in your parents' car, what would it be?

348

If you had to guess which of your friends' kids will grow up with the best attitude toward sex, who would you pick?

If you had to rearrange all the sexual parts of your body, where would you put them?

If you had to have the sexual organs of someone you know, whose would you take?

If you had to name the least restrained person you have ever been to bed with, who would it be?

If you were to have a secret affair in your hometown or city, which hotel would you pick for your rendezvous?

If you had to name the most romantic singer in musical history, who would you pick?

— ✥ —

If you were to name a specific period of your life when you were the horniest, when would it be?

— ✥ —

If you had to name the most consistently sexy dresser of anyone you know, who would you choose?

350

If you had to name one thing you would find most difficult to forgive in your lover, what would it be?

If you were to name a celebrity who is extremely sexy and romantic for their age, who would you pick?

If you had to name the one person you would be most upset by finding out your lover had slept with, who would it be?

If you knew your lover was cheating on you, who is the one person you would be least upset about it being with?

If you had to name the person you know who could do much more with their looks or sex appeal, who would it be?

———— ◄◆► ————

If you had to name the one lover you've had with a specific sexual specialty or talent, but who was not necessarily great in bed otherwise, who would it be?

———— ◄◆► ————

If you could treat each of your parents to a romantic night with anyone in the world, other than each other, who would you pair them with?

———— ◄◆► ————

If you had to name the biggest prude you've ever known, who would it be?

352

If you had to pick the person you think is sexier than everyone seems to realize, who would it be?

If you had to say what's both great and awful about making out in a car, what would it be?

If you had to name the delivery or repair person you'd most like to fool around with, who would you pick?

If you were to name a person who is truly beautiful in all ways, who would you pick?

If you had to name the one thing you least expected to be turned on by but then were, what would it be?

If you had to name the person who is most comfortable with their own sexuality, who would it be?

If you had to name the person who is least comfortable with their own sexuality, who would you pick?

If you could arrange a romantic weekend fling for two people you know who aren't a couple and never will be, who would you pair together, and where would they go?

354

If you had to name a situation where you have used your sensuality to get something other than sex, what would it be?

If you were to use one object every time you masturbated for the rest of your life, what would it be?

If you had to name the most physically demanding lover you ever had, who would it be?

If you were to define "sin" as it relates to sex, what would you say?

355

If you could have one of your sexual fantasies come true tomorrow, what would it be, and how would you prepare for it?

If you had to name the one place (besides bed) that you have masturbated most, where would it be?

If you had to choose the smell you most automatically associate with your lover, what would it be?

If you had to name the most disgusting thing your lover does, what would it be?

356

If you were offered a part in a hard-core porn film, how much money (minimum) would you do it for?

If you could improve your sex life in one way, how would you do it?

If you had to name the dumbest article on love or sex in a magazine that you have read, what would it be?

If you had to name the best advice you've ever heard a sex expert give, what would it be?

357

If you were to name the most surprisingly romantic thing your mate does, what would you say it was?

If you had to name the most difficult good-bye you ever said, what would it be?

━━◆━━

If one of your grown children told you they had acted in a hard-core pornographic video for money, how would you react?

━━◆━━

If your mate suddenly revealed to you that they were now attracted to your opposite sex, what would you say?

If you found out that your favorite political figure had acted in a hard-core porn film when they were very young, how would it affect your opinion or support of them?

If you had to name the one aspect of your own sexuality that you least understand, what would it be?

If you had to name the one lesson of love that took you the longest to learn, what would it be, and why?

If you had to name the most unusual relationship you know of, whose would it be?

359

If you had to have the birthmark of someone you know, whose would you pick?

If you were to describe the perfect amount and form of physical affection you would want every day, what would you say?

If you had to name the one part of your body that you would least want touched by someone you don't like, what would it be?

If you were to choose the most sensual music video you've ever seen, which would you pick?

360

If you could take revenge on any lover from your past, who would it be, and what would you do?

If you could bring one romantic literary character to life and meet them, who would you pick?

If you could go to bed with one person but always wake up with another (of the people you know), who would they be?

If you could guarantee that you will keep one sexual quality (e.g., technique, desire, physical trait) until you die, what would you want it to be?

If you were to buy your lover a sex toy for Christmas, what would you purchase?

If you were to write an ad to put in the personals for a weekend fling, how would you word it?

If you were to read a personal ad for a weekend fling that had the most chance of tempting you, what would it say?

If you could have a platonic nap every day with someone, who would it be with?

362

If you were to pick the moment at which you were the most jealous, when would it be?

If you could make an improvement to condoms in any way, what would you change?

If you were to name the part of your body you would least like to have pierced, what would it be?

If you were to have a phrase tattooed on your lover's privates, what would it say?

If you were to name a person who you believe must be the most satisfied with their sex life, who would you pick?

— ❦ —

If your lover's sexual organ were shaped in the form of a building, which structure would you prefer?

— ❦ —

If you could rent a billboard to say something about love, what would you write, and where would you want it placed?

— ❦ —

If you could make a miniseries about your love life, what would you title it?

364

If you were to name the person you had the most orgasms with in a single session of lovemaking, who would win?

If you had to wear one article of clothing you already own every time you went out on a date in the future, what would you select?

If you wanted to revive a flagging physical relationship, how would you go about it?

If you had to name the biggest sexual braggart you've ever known, who would it be?

365

If your lover could lose one inhibition, what would you want it to be?

If you could be bolder in one area of your love life, what would you pick?

If one physical part of you could be bigger, what would it be?

If one physical part of you could be smaller, what would you choose?

If you could create a bouquet of flowers for your loved one, what would it be made up of?

—————— ✠ ——————

If your naked body were to be lathered with a certain kind of dessert, what would it be?

—————— ✠ ——————

If you were to direct an erotic love scene for a film, what would it include?

—————— ✠ ——————

If you could lose one inhibition, which would you choose?

367

If you could give someone a hickey in any shape and size, who would receive it, and on what part of the body?

If you were to give a new permanent body marking to your lover, what would it be, and where?

If at the height of passion your lover were to whisper or yell something, what would you want it to be?

If someone were to seduce you in a foreign language, which would you choose?

If you had to name the smallest space you've ever had sex in, where was it?

If you had to name a really naughty thing you've done at someone else's wedding, what would it be?

— ✦ —

If you had to pick the nationality of people that you find the most attractive, which would it be?

— ✦ —

If you could have one thing installed beside your bed, what would you want?

If you could have one part of your body glow in the dark, what part would it be?

—————≡◆≡—————

If your lover were to leave you now, what one thing would you want them to leave behind for you to remember them by?

If you could do one great trick with your tongue that you can't now do, what would it be?

—————≡◆≡—————

If you could determine the size and shape of your lover's sexual organs, what would they be?

370

If you had to name the most erotic piece of artwork you've ever seen, what would you choose?

If you had to name the one thing that should turn you on in bed but just never does, what would it be?

If you were to describe the one natural setting you'd most like to make love in, what would it be like?

If you could have only one sexual fantasy—repeatedly—for the rest of your life, what would it involve?

If you had to choose a foreign accent that you find sexy, what would you say?

⎯⎯ ⚊◆⚊ ⎯⎯

If you had to name the worst thing you ever said to a lover in a heated moment, what was it?

⎯⎯ ⚊◆⚊ ⎯⎯

If you were to name the people you know who have been married the longest, who would they be?

⎯⎯ ⚊◆⚊ ⎯⎯

If you were to name the person you know who was married for the shortest time, who would win?

If you could learn one thing about your parents' honeymoon, what would you want to know?

✦

If you had to recall your very first sexual thought, what would you say it was?

✦

If you were caught by your children in bed having sex, what would you say (in one sentence)?

If you were to name the most sensual perfume on the market, which scent would win?

If you had to name the person who has the worst taste in girl-friends or boyfriends, who would it be?

If you were to recall the most romantic evening you have had that did not involve sex, what would it be?

If you could have anyone you know tuck you into bed every night with a single kiss, who would you pick?

If you could teach your kids one thing about romance, what would you tell them?

If you were to kiss the toes of anyone in the world, whose would you choose?

If you had to include one animal in your next lovemaking, what kind would it be?

If you had to name the person who has been most deceived by their mate, who would you select?

If you could interview any porn star, who would you pick, and what would your first question be?

If you could have an existing law related to sex eliminated, what would it be?

If you were to describe the sexiest bathing suit you've seen, what would you say?

If you had to say one word every time you had an orgasm, what word would you pick?

If you had to describe the intimate details of each of your sexual encounters to one person you know platonically, who would you pick?

If you were to be sent to a prostitute who had been already paid, what would you do with them?

If you were to pick the least sexy fashion trend of your lifetime, what would it be?

If you were to pick the period with the sexiest fashions during your lifetime, what would win?

If for the rest of your life you could have a single thing delivered to your bed right after you had sex (besides money), what would you want it to be?

If you had to pick the most affectionate type of animal, what would it be?

If you could have been the mistress or lover of any great figure from history, who would you pick?

If you were to have an orgy with any six people you know, who would you invite?

If you had to make love listening to the same piece of music for the rest of your life, what would you select?

If you could have stood up one person you should have, who would it be?

———❖———

If you were to name the language that sounds the most romantic, which would it be?

———❖———

If you could go back and change one thing about your honeymoon, what would it be?

If you were to name the best speech or toast you have heard at someone's wedding, who gave it, and what did they say?

If you were trying to be a matchmaker for two people you know, how would you do it?

If you could have only one person say "I love you" to you, who would you want it to be?

If you were to describe your overall sex life (from your first experience through your most recent), what would you say?

If you were to name a place where you would like to masturbate that you never have, what would it be?

380

If you could rewrite your marriage vows, how would you change them?

If you were to advise someone on the perfect way to elope, what would you say?

If you were to name the one thing that makes you feel sexy, what would it be?

If you were to come up with one positive result of a mate cheating on their spouse, what would it be?

If you had to name one sexual thing you pray that your lover will never ask you to do, what would it be?

If you could have any sculpture come alive to make love to, which piece would you want?

If there was one thing relating to your love life that you could be blackmailed for, what would it be?

If you were to dedicate any single thing to someone to show your love for them, what would it be, and to whom?

382

If you were to have a baby with someone with whom you could never have a relationship, whose child would you want?

If you could have sex with one pagan god, which would it be?

＊＊＊

If you could produce a film about safe sex for kids, what would it be like?

＊＊＊

If you had to pick a book title that most accurately sums up your love life, what would it be?

383

If you were to recall the time when you ruined the most clothes during the heat of passion, when would you say it was?

If you could meet the love of your life, where would you want the meeting to take place?

If you were the opposite sex for a year, what one sexual thing would you never do with a lover?

If you were to have a dead loved one as an inanimate object in your house, what would they be?

384

If you found out that your mate had once acted in a hard-core pornographic film, what would you do or say to them (and would you want to see it)?

If you had to name the most beautiful or impressive wedding or engagement ring you have ever seen, whose would it be?

If you could give one piece of sexual advice to the opposite gender, what would it be?

If you could give one piece of sexual advice to your own gender, what would it be?

385

If you had to recall the most shocking thing you have accidently seen going on between two people, what would it be?

If you could dedicate one work of art to someone you love, which would it be, and to whom would you dedicate it?

If you were to die for someone for the sake of love, who would you die for?

If you had to identify the darkest fictional character that you find erotic and sensual, who would it be?

If you could learn one dance to turn your lover on, what would you pick?

⚊⚬⚊

If you could only kiss your lover on one spot of their body forevermore, what spot would you choose?

⚊⚬⚊

If you could give Dr. Ruth one piece of sexual advice, what would you say?

⚊⚬⚊

If you could make love with your current lover, and include one lover from your past in the fun, who would you pick?

387

If you were to name a nonsexual thing that always arouses you, what would it be?

━━◆━━

If you were to recite any poem to your present lover, which would you choose?

━━◆━━

If you wanted to get the love of your life to fall in love with you, to what extremes would you go?

━━◆━━

If you found out the love of your life had only one month to live, how would you spend your time with them?

388

If you could say "I love you" only one more time, who would you say it to?

If you could send your parents on a second honeymoon anywhere in the world, all expenses paid, where would you like it to be?

If you had to make love under a giant photograph of one member of your family, who would you want it to be, and who wouldn't you want it to be?

If you had to define "love" in a few simple words, how would you do it?

EVELYN MCFARLANE was born in Brooklyn and grew up in San Diego. She received a degree in architecture from Cornell University and has worked in New York and Boston. She is now living in Florence, Italy, and spends her time painting and writing.

JAMES SAYWELL was born in Canada. He studied architecture in Toronto and at Princeton, and he designs buildings and furniture, paints, writes, and teaches architecture. He divides his time between the United States and Italy.